CREATING CALM

AMIDST THE STORM

CREATING CALM

AMIDST THE STORM

How to Have Retirement Certainty
Even in Uncertain Times

PHILLIS SAX PILVINIS

Advantage®

Published by Advantage, Charleston, South Carolina.
Member of Advantage Media Group.

ADVANTAGE is a registered trademark and the Advantage colophon is a trademark of Advantage Media Group, Inc.

Printed in the United States of America.

ISBN: 978-159932-312-1
LCCN: 2013932182

This publication is designed to provide accurate and authoritative information in regard to the subject matter covered. It is sold with the understanding that the publisher is not engaged in rendering legal, accounting, or other professional services. If legal advice or other expert assistance is required, the services of a competent professional person should be sought.

Advantage Media Group is proud to be a part of the Tree Neutral® program. Tree Neutral offsets the number of trees consumed in the production and printing of this book by taking proactive steps such as planting trees in direct proportion to the number of trees used to print books. To learn more about Tree Neutral, please visit www.treeneutral.com. To learn more about Advantage's commitment to being a responsible steward of the environment, please visit www.advantagefamily.com/green

Advantage Media Group is a publisher of business, self-improvement, and professional development books and online learning. We help entrepreneurs, business leaders, and professionals share their Stories, Passion, and Knowledge to help others Learn & Grow™. Do you have a manuscript or book idea that you would like us to consider for publishing? Please visit advantagefamily.com or call 1.866.775.1696.

TABLE OF CONTENTS

FOREWORD

Congratulations!

Opening this book is your first step toward taking control of your retirement. If you're like most preretirees and retirees, you have concerns about your retirement or want to confirm you are on the right track. Well, I'm honored to be the one to tell you, in my professional opinion, you are looking for guidance in the right place. There are more than 300,000 financial advisors in the country, but only a select few have joined an elite group that has devoted extensive time and energy to develop their expertise in retirement and estate planning. Phillis is one of these leaders.

Although I have a successful CPA practice, more than a decade ago I dedicated my energy to educating people and financial advisors on the correct way to do IRA tax planning and distribution. In 2005 I started Ed Slott's Elite IRA Advisor Group, of which Phillis is a charter master member. This group undergoes rigorous training and mentoring on an ongoing basis to learn the essentials necessary to help their clients navigate safely through the myriad of ever-changing IRS rules and regulations and avoid excessive taxation.

In the ten years I have known Phillis, I am continually impressed with her passion, dedication, and expertise to successfully help people with their retirement and income planning. As a financial advisor, Phillis has demonstrated her professional commitment and discipline to stay current in our industry and acquire the specialized training and education critical to manage and secure your wealth.

I am confident this book will be an invaluable resource to you in creating certainty in your retirement.

—Ed Slott

Ed Slott has been named "the best source for IRA advice" by the *Wall Street Journal* and is a nationally recognized IRA-distribution expert, professional speaker, and creator of several public television specials, including *Ed Slott's Retirement Rescue!* viewed by millions of Americans.

ACKNOWLEDGMENTS

As passionate and verbose about my beliefs as I am, I always thought that writing a book would be a piece of cake. I am now humbled. It is not as easy as a good best seller would have you think. However, once all is typed, edited, and printed, I just may write another one. It's been a great experience to develop and share my best ideas to help you find a deeper calm in the midst of your retirement planning, knowing your finances are secure. If one thing I wrote helped you achieve that freedom, I will be satisfied. Of course, I didn't do this work alone. My appreciation belongs to many colleagues, friends, and family for their support and advice, but a few most especially.

My first acknowledgments—and those most bittersweet—are for my wonderful parents, Myer and Sandra Sax. Though I lost them from this world too soon, I know how very proud they would be of this achievement. It's true they were loving parents and supportive of my career. However, it is the trajectory of their lives that is the impetus and inspiration behind this book. In my life, this adage rings true: every bad experience brings something of value to cherish and put to good purpose. My dad's unexpected death at the age of fifty-nine awoke a fierce instinct within me to protect my mom from any more heartache, and that included shielding her finances. Fourteen years later, my mom's tragic accident convinced me of the comfort and kindness of such planning. My passion to specialize in preservation and income planning for retirement took root in these events and today compels me to ensure that my clients have the best financial protection from life's uncertainties. With their spirits beside me, I honor my parents' foresight and love, and do my best to put both to good purpose in this book and in my work.

It is also my hope that I have not scared off my family and associates with the promise (or is it a threat?) of another book. My gratitude is owed to many who have encouraged, guided and cajoled me through this process, but three in particular I must single out. Because I want many anniversaries to come, first let me thank Harry, my darling husband of almost thirty years for being a wonderful father to our two beautiful children, a patient partner, and most especially for standing by me through thick or thin, tantrums or tears, triumphs and losses, with loyalty and love. Secondly, I thank my vice president of operations, radio cohost, and most importantly, dear friend, Jill Spencer. Her input, humor and camaraderie, support and push are a big reason I could stay with this project. She is always "just Jill," and she is always the best! Finally, I give much appreciation to my good friend of many decades and adventures, Kathy Ouellette, for her eleventh-hour editing assistance to help my words flow. Without these three very special people, completing *Creating Calm Amidst the Storm* would have been much more tumultuous, a lot more tedious, and definitely not as polished or fun.

While we should always hope for the best, planning for the worst is a true act of loving kindness for our loved ones. It is my intent that these ideas take root and bear fruit and shelter in abundance for you in your life. From my heart to yours, may this simple book help you plan and live a better retirement.

WHY THIS BOOK?

WHY THIS BOOK?

Every day, I work with people on the verge of, or settling into, their retirement. This is a milestone they have worked toward their whole lives, and it is a transition that can bring as many fears and confusions as it will new freedoms. After spending more than thirty years in this field, I wanted to write a book that would help make people's retirement planning simple and empowering, a book that would demystify the complicated landscape of regulations, products, and mixed messages surrounding this important phase of life. I felt especially compelled to write this book because of the tremendously uncertain and chaotic times that our generation of retirees and up-and-coming retirees are facing (and yes, I am one of them).

For the first time in American history, thousands of baby boomers are arriving at the ordained retirement age in rapid succession. On January 1, 2011, more than 7,000 baby boomers reached the age of sixty-five. This is going to keep happening every single day for the next nineteen years.[1] The once-dependable Social Security system is teetering because of an unprecedented demand for payouts, poor fiscal management, fiscal cliffs, and a stormy economy. No one knows what benefits or cost-of-living increases can be counted on or for how long. Inflation is rising. Taxes are

---

1   United States Census Bureau.

rising. Pensions are diminishing or becoming nonexistent. Who would have ever thought, for example, that GM and Ford would need to unload billions of dollars in pension obligations to limit the risk associated with managing pension plans?[2] Furthermore, the government seems to be waging a war against American savers, as shown by the low interest rates and volatile stock market.

The good news is people are living longer; the bad news is people are living longer. This means you need to plan for a longer retirement and anticipate the outrageous costs of health care in case of a catastrophic illness. Compounding these fears are the turbulent stock market, which is stressed by trillions of dollars of unsustainable national debt, and the unstable global economy. These looming problems are overwhelming and troublesome for all of us. Yet even in the midst of this uncertainty, you have a tremendous opportunity to protect and preserve your life's earnings. With a well-planned and realistic financial map, you can have certainty of income, assurance that you will not outlive your money, and freedom to live your life independently. You can have calm amidst the storm, and this book will show you how.

WHY TRUST WHAT I SAY?

First, let me briefly share my background and experience so you will know why you should consider taking advice from me. I started my career in the financial planning industry more than thirty years ago with the John Hancock Insurance Company. I was right out of college and just twenty-two years old. I earned my securities and insurance licenses within my first year of employment. Very quickly, I realized that my passion was to help young people plan for retire-

2   "GM outsources pensions, offers lump-sum buyouts," *USA Today*, June 1, 2012.

ment, and one great tool for that was a well-kept secret found within the guarantees of a life insurance plan. I made it my mission to share this secret with as many people as I could, and I accomplished this with such force that within the year I was appointed manager and became responsible for a ten-agent office.

Five years later, my husband and I started a family, and I happily became a stay-at-home mom who raised our two children for the next eleven years. In between the

With a well-planned and realistic financial map, you can have certainty of income, assurance that you will not outlive your money, and freedom to live your life independently.

diapering, dinners, soccer games, and family times, when the kids were at school or in bed, I took out my financial books or went online to research and study the current trends and best practices of my industry. I spent as much time trading in the stock market as my son did playing his videos games, and I read anything I could get my hands on—right or left, good or bad—to ensure that I was considering all approaches, nuances, and logic to managing, investing, and protecting money.

Toward the end of my maternal hiatus, a deeply tragic event changed my life and my ideas about retirement planning. My father, who was fifty-nine, was killed instantly in an automobile accident, leaving my mom a very young widow. My parents were average, hard-working people from New Jersey who followed the mores of their generation. My dad had his own kitchen and bath remodeling business, and my mom was a stay-at-home mom who had raised my brother and me. Dad took care of the finances and Mom took care of the family. While my dad had always been a believer in the value of a life insurance policy, a few years into my career he and I had sat down and discussed how much more insurance he needed to fully protect my mom in case he died. I showed him how an increased contract would double as a good accumulation plan and be a living benefit to him as much as it would provide adequate survivor protection for my mom. My dad purchased the policy. Because of that choice, after his death, my mom had the instant nest egg that my dad had always planned to have saved in time for their "golden years."

At this juncture, I had an epiphany. My mom had never worked outside the home; she had no resume, college education, or confidence with which to enter the job market easily. I realized that because my mom did not have a paycheck, she had to keep that insurance money. She was a relatively young, healthy woman who could live for many years, and that money had to last. I realized that she was just like every other person transitioning into or already in retirement, a situation in which the rules about investing change. Here she was at this crossroads, and she was encountering this huge gap between understanding these rules and knowing what goals were best for her money. My dad passed away in 1991. If you remember, this was at a time when the stock market was going up and up. Most people were investing the majority of their assets, not to mention their loose change, and they watched as their portfolios increased beyond their wildest dreams.

Contrary to the trends of that time, I advised my mom to put her money in more conservative investments. Most of my mom's friends thought she was nuts for not being in the market, but the lion's share of her money was money she needed to keep and could not afford to lose. She did not have time to recover and did not have a paycheck to make up any losses. While her friends were doubling and tripling their money in the stock market, my mom was earning a smaller, decent rate of return that posed little risk to her principal. I had absolute conviction that we had to first and foremost protect her life savings and grow it safely. I knew in my heart that my mom was just like many other retirees: if she earned a lot on that money, her lifestyle would not change, while the loss of that money would devastate her remaining life's quality and choices. Truth be told, along came the year 2000, and we know the rest of the story. My mom's friends lost money that they could not afford to lose. She never lost a night's sleep over such a problem regarding her finances and maintained an independent lifestyle on her own terms.

Having lived through that experience, I became certain I could make the greatest impact on people's lives by guiding them through the transition from the first phase of their life (the accumulation or working years) into the second phase of their life (the preservation or retirement phase). In my thirty years of retirement planning, during which time I have worked with hundreds of people, I have seen over and over that most people do not realize that the rules regarding their money totally change for retirement. They also do not understand that their mindset needs to change too. For all of us, old habits die hard. Yet people must make critical changes to their attitudes and strategies in order to be prepared for retirement and then comfortably retired. Many hard-working people save sufficiently for retirement, but fail to make the adjustments necessary to secure those funds. As a result, they make critical mistakes with their nest eggs that cost them dearly. What I want those of you who are reading this book to know is that *once you shift into a "retirement attitude" and acquire a basic grounding in the rules for being retirement-prepared, you will—without fail—avoid painful and irrevocable mistakes with your life's savings.* And I want to help you make these changes in the right way.

THE VALUE OF INDEPENDENT ADVICE

At first, in my new approach to retirement planning, I focused on helping people protect their retirement dollars from the impact of a catastrophic illness until I realized that such an event was just a piece of that bigger retirement-planning picture. I realized that in order to be able to encompass a 360-degree view and address the full spectrum of clients' needs, I needed to become an independent advisor.

Originally, John Hancock, Metropolitan, and essentially all of the financial planning companies were relatively the same: they offered similar products, strategies, and costs. However, the world changed, and today not all companies are the same. Their offers may seem similar on the surface, but when you delve into the details, you will find subtle distinctions that make a difference. In other words, the devil is in the details, and there can be hell to pay if you do not pay close attention to the fine print. To help more people, I launched my own company as an independent advisor dedicated to working specifically with baby boomers and retirees.

My position as an independent advisor significantly increases the value I bring to my clients. I customize solutions for my clients, first by listening to their goals, and second by designing a unique plan for each one, selecting those companies, products, and/or investments that best meet a client's specific needs. Not all products and/or investments are created equal, and my extensive knowledge and direct experience of which products and strategies perform best—regardless of the company—ensures that my clients receive comprehensive, unbiased, and innovative recommendations handpicked to match each individual's unique financial situation. My clients are not going to know every product or investment opportunity in the marketplace and the differences between them, but I do.

Eventually, I gave up my brokerage license and became a Series 65 registered investment advisor for a very important reason. As an investment advisor, I am held to a higher standard of accountability—that of a fiduciary—while a broker is held only to a standard of suitability. *Suitability* means that the recommendation is reasonable, but it does not have to be the best or most cost-efficient choice. In contrast, a fiduciary always has the responsibility of serving his or her clients' best interests first and is required to make a recommendation of the most ideal investment. As an investment advisor, I am not transaction oriented, as opposed to brokers, who are only paid when they buy or sell on a client's behalf. Unlike a broker, I am not paid commissions, so there can never be a conflict of interest when I make recommendations. Here is how I am paid: I either receive a percentage based on the amount of client assets I manage, or I am paid a specific fee. I believe this system is a huge advantage to my clients and much fairer to them too, since everything is transparent and there is no hidden agenda. I am not trying to sell a client a product based on a company's commission to me. Instead, I am recommending the best vehicle that matches the client's personal retirement goals. Moreover, I am investing right along with the client in order to ensure that it is successful.

BECOME THE CEO OF YOUR MONEY

This book is intended for the person who wants to take control of his or her retirement destiny. It is crucial for you to understand that the buck stops with you. Your money is your responsibility, and there is nobody on earth with more vested interest in how that money is controlled. If I had a nickel for everybody who came into my office and told me, "My CPA did not tell me I could save money on this," or "My stockbroker did not take me out of the market in time," I would have a lot of nickels. Everybody else is responsible—and I get it. We rely on other people. If something falls into their area of expertise, we should be entitled to rely on them to a certain degree. The fact of the matter is that, while you can blame whomever you want, if you surrender control of and responsibility for your money, it is your retirement that suffers and nobody else's. If you are not interested in taking responsibility for managing your funds, this is the wrong book for you. However, if you recognize the importance of being the CEO of your own money—and you should—this book will help you to plan ahead to maximize opportunities and nimbly sidestep the potential pitfalls. Surprisingly, perhaps, this is not as difficult to do as you may think.

There are many things in this world that we cannot control. For example, we cannot control tax rates, tax increases, or which items are taxed. We cannot control whether we are going to have a major health crisis or, for that matter, what the costs for health care will be. We certainly cannot control whether the market is going to go up or down; we are a part of a global economy that is under a constant barrage of variables.

What we can control is where we put our money, how we access it in retirement, and who will receive it after we pass on. In this book I will discuss the things you can control in this crazy, shook-up world. I am going to guide you toward the retirement of your dreams and on to the path that will get you there. Once you own your retirement, you can take simple steps to guarantee it works for you, not the other way around. Understanding the rules of the retirement system as they apply to your investments and savings is the first step toward taking control of the things you can affect. Implementing this knowledge will ensure that, for the rest of your life, you enjoy the quality of life to which you have become accustomed.

Some of the crucial areas that I am going to cover in this book include the following:

- Determining what financial phase you are in, and how you can plan differently for each phase;
- Deciding when you should start to transition from the accumulation phase to the preservation phase;
- Identifying some ways in which you can reduce and even eliminate taxes;
- Determining how much financial risk you should be taking, now and in retirement;
- Planning how you can position your money for safety;
- Discovering hidden fees you may be paying on your investments and how to reduce or eliminate them;
- Planning for retiring in a pensionless society by creating your own income plan with safe money accounts;
- Learning what Wall Street does not want you to know; and
- Finding out how to build the right team of professionals who will guide you through the proper steps to the retirement of your dreams.

The fact is most people do not know where to turn for trustworthy and unbiased information about their retirement planning. You are not alone in your search for answers to your questions about how to step into retirement and live through it with the assurance that you will not have a moment's lost sleep because of your finances.

I am confident that this book will provide you with some tools you can use to demystify the overwhelming, and often conflicting information that competes for your attention. This book will equip you with skills and knowledge that will give you the power, confidence, and serenity to walk into and enjoy a secure retirement. It is my goal to see you successfully take control and protect those life savings that represent years of hard work, sacrifice, and perseverance so that you will have a **greater sense of calm as you ride through the storm of these chaotic and uncertain times.**

THE THREE-LEGGED STOOL

Whatever You Do, Do Not Sit on It

THE THREE-LEGGED STOOL

Whatever You Do, Do Not Sit on It

Have you ever seen a three-legged stool? It is a surprisingly sturdy piece of furniture that can bear a lot of weight safely—as long as all three legs are sound. Let one leg come off, however, and the whole thing collapses.

Historically, our government has encouraged people thinking about retirement to use a structure very much like a three-legged stool. In previous years, the first leg of the stool was Social Security. Our government sponsored this form of mandatory savings, or pension system of sorts, and told people they could safely rely on it. The second leg was the defined pension plan, an employee benefit provided by many large, private companies. Each company would pay in to a pool of funds, invest in the pool, and then guarantee employees a defined benefit upon retirement, regardless of how the market performed. With a defined pension, people knew the exact amount they would receive from their company upon retirement, and they could use this to supple-

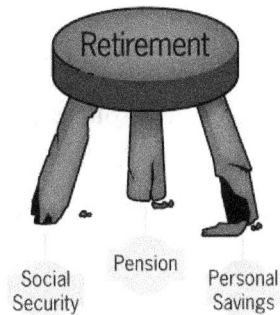

ment their social security benefits. The third leg was personal savings that people set aside along the way for additional security and peace of mind. In the 1950s, after a devastating depression and World War II, most people were disciplined stewards of their money, conscious that deprivation and rationing could be just around the corner.

Today, those legs are collapsing. How plausible is it that you can rely on Social Security to be there for your retirement? According to the Social Security Trustees' *2012 Annual Report*, because Peter has been robbed to pay Paul, "the fund that helps finance benefits for 44 million senior citizens and survivors of deceased workers will be exhausted by 2035."[3] With a cost of living increase totaling 3.6 percent over the past three years,[4] the likelihood of incurring substantial cost-of-living adjustments (COLA) in the future is, in my opinion, questionable. Social Security, which the government always meant to be only a supplemental income during people's retirement, an addition to other streams of revenue that employers bestowed and/or that people diligently put in place, has now become too many people's only source of retirement income. This source is headed for increasingly diminished returns. It is a shaky leg, at best.

Once upon a time, the second leg, the defined pension plan, was a flagship benefit that employers unfurled to guarantee employees' loyalty. In addition to that gold watch upon retirement, each employee could count on a fixed payout the day he or she traded the carpool for a golf cart or garden bench. Today, defined benefit plans are headed toward extinction, priced out of existence by exorbitant costs. Defined-contribution plans, such as 401(k) accounts, are much less expensive. Increasingly, such plans are the only retirement benefits offered by private companies. A defined-contribution

---

3　Social Security Trustees, *2012 Annual Report.*

4　Social Security Administration (www.ssa.gov).

plan is basically a 401(k), a plan in which the only certain thing is how much you contribute. Quite frankly, the outcome of this vehicle depends entirely upon the whims of the stock market, and take into consideration the fact that employees are now expected to be their own pension managers, responsible for picking and choosing from a small selection of investment options (usually costly mutual funds with significant fees and no guarantees). A defined-contribution plan is not exactly the Queen Mary II of pension plans.

The third leg probably wobbles the most. Today, people just are not stockpiling personal savings as they did thirty or forty years ago. The baby boomers either do not have the discipline to sacrifice their immediate wants, or they are struggling just to make ends meet, hold off foreclosures, or pay rising tuition for their college-enrolled kids (that is, if they are not subsidizing the kids' move back home because the job market is so tough). If these potential retirees have been diligent in saving, they encounter dismal interest rates, which generate much lower returns. This situation makes a mattress seem a viable place to store cash. The stock market's rollercoaster ride may provide more chills than thrills to anyone seeking growth opportunities.

The upshot of the loss of these guarantees is that people are approaching and entering retirement without anything solid to replace the income a steady paycheck always provided. That is a precarious, unsettling place to be.

With the traditional three-legged stool nearing obsolescence, if not entirely breaking beyond repair, people need to keep their eyes wide open and try to prevent distressing eleventh-hour newsflashes. Now is the time to align your financial preparations with current economic indicators, all while anticipating the worst, and build a steady stool of your own making.

To haphazardly save or not to save money is not the question to be asking in these times. Even Hamlet would agree that to avoid the slings and arrows of outrageous retirement misfortunes, savings and plans for every contingency are formidable arms to bear against a pending sea of troubles.[5]

Far too often, I see people who do not understand how to invest their money in order to replace the paychecks that will stop upon their retirement. I cover this topic every week on my radio show to ensure that my listeners are exposed to ideas and opportunities that will keep them from being caught unaware without enough time to make positive changes to address their financial problems.

If you would like to listen to my past radio shows, **Living Your Life with Phillis Sax Pilvinis,** *broadcast on* **AM960 The Patriot** *every Sunday at 11 am, please visit my website at* **www.pspassoc.com** *for a list of archived recordings.*

Rather than design and stick to a solid plan that ensures a successful retirement, too many people **hope** that their retirement accounts are going to be enough to carry them through to a natural death. Too many people **hope** that the market is going to rise and build their assets for them. Just as many people **hope** that the market will not have fallen when they bid their colleagues goodbye and head to the bank to deposit that last company paycheck. The retirees and preretirees out there have

---

5   With apologies to Mr. Shakespeare.

a great deal of hope, but not nearly enough certainty. Today, that three-legged piece of retirement furniture, once a reliable footstool upon which you could rest your weary legs after a long career, is best viewed as a piece of vintage Americana: it has lots of good memories but is too fragile for use. Today is the best day to take control of your destiny and, with your eyes wide open, build a solid retirement plan. The old cliché rings true: while people do not plan to fail, far too many fail to plan.

Knowing the state of American footstools, I urge you to take up a hammer, grab some nails, and craft your own stool. Put aside your hopes that the market is going to be as good as it was in the '90s. Stop drinking the Wall Street Kool-Aid that seduces you to believe that the market always comes back. Instead, work with more secure and stable options available to you and build a realistic plan.

Let me show you the simple steps you need to take in order to accomplish these goals.

THE THREE
FINANCIAL PHASES

Assuring Safe Passage to Retirement and Beyond

THE THREE FINANCIAL PHASES

Assuring Safe Passage to Retirement and Beyond

It's important to remember that there are three defined financial phases you will encounter during your lifetime: **accumulation, preservation, and distribution**. Each phase requires you to use a different strategy that considers that phase's unique opportunities and requirements. Therefore, it stands to reason that there are different types of advisors whose areas of expertise are better suited to help you navigate through one phase than another. Just as there are specialists in the medical profession, there are specialists in the financial profession. Choosing the right one at the right stage is vital to your retirement success.

PHASE I: THE ACCUMULATION
STAGE OR WORKING YEARS

The first financial stage is the **accumulation stage**. This stage covers your working years, usually a span of time averaging forty years, when you have a regular paycheck coming in the door. Specifically, the accumulation phase covers your working years from age twenty to the average age of retirement, which is about sixty-four today.[6] During this time, maybe you are raising a family, paying a mortgage, climbing the career ladder, paying for tuition or weddings, or splurging on the occasional vacation. Fueling whatever you do during this period is that weekly paycheck and the fact that time is before you. With lots of years and paychecks ahead, it is prudent to take a portion of your earnings and put it away for your retirement years. Because time is on your side, and because you have a more than sufficient paycheck to cover the household bills coming at you every few minutes, you can afford to take some risks with these savings and invest them in the stock market. Historically, stocks do outperform other types of investment vehicles over the long term. During the accumulation phase, strategic market investing is a good thing, as long as you are investing systematically, have enough time on your side, and use what is clearly long-term money. In today's volatile market, "enough time" is at least fifteen years.

The accumulation stage is when you, as the CEO of your money, prepare a budget that determines how much you can realistically and consistently invest for the long term. Once you arrive at an accurate figure of what you can truly afford to put aside and you have the discipline to follow through, you are ready to work with an accumulation specialist. Typically, this is the kind of advisor who spends his or her days sitting in front of the computer, looking at all the stocks, bonds, and mutual funds available, and who is knowledgeable enough to help you pick and choose the best ones. This advisor's goal is growth for you at any cost.

When interviewing advisors for the accumulation phase, or any phase, make sure they demonstrate one essential skill: the ability to listen

---

6   Center for Retirement Research, Boston College. Anthony Webb, from the Center for Retirement Research, appeared as a guest on my radio show. We had a very interesting discussion about how someone should determine at what age he or she is ready to take the plunge into retirement.

to and hear your goals, not just to persuade you to theirs. Do not settle for anything less. This skill indicates the telltale distinction between a sales pitch and true advice. It is also in your best interest to do a complete background check and verify how the advisors are licensed and to which organizations they belong. Ask them questions about their continuing education and current reading in their particular niche. Financial planning is a dynamic market. Advisors who do not stay on top of their industry could mislead you, quite unintentionally, and take you down a dark alley that leads to poor outcomes.

In the accumulation stage, you set the foundation that will determine the possible choices and outcomes for your next two financial stages. If you become a good saver early in your working life and invest your savings wisely, you will be amazed by how powerfully your cumulative years of saving will impact your compounding investments; a twenty-year-old needs to put away much, much less than a fifty-year-old, for example, in order to become a millionaire by age sixty.

Let me add a little caveat here: if you have been successful at saving and have accumulated a nice nest egg, it is prudent, even critical, to begin preparations for your retirement five to ten years before your desired retirement target age. This is the big aha moment when it is time to align with a second type of financial advisor, one who will secure your portfolio with leading-edge strategies unique to current economic times and your specific goals. This preservation- and income-driven specialist is your wealth manager. In other words, the accumulation specialist gets you to the Promised Land, after which you need the guidance of a preservation- and income-driven specialist to ensure you live a comfortable and a financially secure life in that land.

This is an area in which you should exert the full powers invested in you as CEO of your money by taking charge of selecting your advisor. Unfortunately, my industry is not structured like the medical industry. What I mean by this is that in the medical profession it is normal procedure for a general practitioner to refer you to a specialist when a diagnosis is outside the former's realm of expertise. If you have a heart problem, the general practitioner is going to refer you to a cardiologist. However, in my profession an accumulation specialist is not going to refer a client to someone like me, the preservation- and income-driven specialist. Why? Accumulation specialists will not make such a recommendation because doing so is tantamount to firing themselves. They will take a pay cut. Instead, it becomes incumbent upon you to make that monumental transition. Remember, this is something within your control.

Shifting your mindset from the accumulation phase to the preservation stage, ahead of your retirement date, gives you the opportunity to adjust or stop current financial strategies and begin the transition toward those that will most benefit your next phase. It is important that you do not wait until the eleventh hour to do this; at that time, it will be more challenging to unscramble any deficits in your nest egg. If you plan to retire at sixty-four, the ideal time to begin these steps is at fifty-four years of age—no later than fifty-nine. Over the years, I have had too many people come into my office and say, "Phillis, I was going to retire next year because my 401(k) was doing so well—but then it went down! Now my 401(k) is a 101(k), and I do not know when I will be able to retire." Think about that. Isn't that disturbing? When you only have five to ten years in as volatile a market as today's is, time is no longer your friend. There is not enough time in which you can compound enough funds to replace that paycheck. It is mathematically impossible.

While you certainly cannot control what the market is going to do, you can control the following: how much of your surplus dollars you save, where you choose to invest those dollars, and who helps you make these choices. It is imperative to realize the importance of taking that control early on and ensuring that you integrate a carefully calculated five- to ten-year transition plan for your retirement into your accumulation plan while you are still working and investing. The sooner you engage in these actions during your working years, the more secure your transition to retirement will be.

PHASE II: THE PRESERVATION STAGE: TRANSITIONING INTO AND THROUGH THE RETIREMENT YEARS

The second financial phase is the **preservation phase.** This is the time when it becomes crucial that you take care of and preserve the money that you were diligent enough to put away when you were still receiving a paycheck. The money you now have consists of any stable income pensions you have been granted, your Social Security benefits, and any monies you have saved. By this point, I hope, you have built your nest egg sufficiently, since whatever you have accumulated up to this point must last you for the rest of your life.

Let me explain some of the important differences between the accumulation and preservation financial phases. Throughout the accumulation phase, your primary objective is your money's growth. You measure its progress by asking yourself what return you are getting on your money. That is the end goal, and that is where the bragging rights are. Trouble happens in the preservation stage when people continue to view their money as if they were still in the accumulation phase. They act without duly considering that they may soon encounter a pressing need to spend a chunk of that money, and they forget that this sum will not be replaced by another paycheck. If investments are down at that time, which they very well could be, the result is that they have even less money to stretch through their retired years. That, my friend, is dangerous. That spells disaster. You need to realize that you do not get a second chance with these funds; the clock runs down and there is no new income, no reliable paycheck, with which to replenish its loss.

During the preservation stage, you should be focused on identifying the potential risks to your accumulated money and implementing actions to mitigate the greatest threats. Realize that risk can emerge from uncertainty in financial markets, health crises, accidents, family emergencies, and acts of nature, among other events. Anticipating possible scenarios that could consume your savings and having a plan or reasonable solution in place to address it will go a long way toward protecting your resources, which cannot be replenished. One major threat, for example, is having too much money in the market when the market hits an inevitable downturn. When that happens, you do not have that money. How do you get it back? Do you go to Vegas and roll the dice? Do you give it to a broker who thinks he is Houdini?

I want to shout from the rooftops how important it is to focus on protecting this money and safeguarding it from all the things that can take it away.

The above are chancy ideas at best. The sad fact is that you may never get that money back, not in your lifetime. Your nest egg has to be sufficient to cover whatever shortfall might exist between your ability, when retired, to meet your income needs and your income wants. I want to shout from the rooftops how important it is to focus on protecting this money and safeguarding it from all the things that can take it away. Remember, whatever you have accumulated has to last you the rest of your life, no matter how long that is. Your strategy is not about doubling or tripling your money at this stage; your strategy should be about keeping that money. The important thing is to have in place a solid plan that identifies all the threats to your money and protects your money from them. While the above may seem redundant, I want to stress how important this topic is.

The first step of a good preservation plan is to consider and choose a logical retirement date. A clearly identified timeframe is crucial for you in determining which strategies you will be able to implement within this period. Today, people often assume that the minute they hit that magic age—sixty-two or sixty-five—they can automatically retire. They have no pension. They have a 401(k) riding in a capricious market, and that money is, quite possibly, the majority of their nest egg. They have no other contingency plans. Yet, they arrive at this heralded milestone assuming they can and should retire, and they expect that enough money to cover the costs of living for the next twenty years or so will somehow be there. They come to my office, and together we start painting their picture of retirement. Then, and only then, do they realize that if living in a cardboard box on the street is their idea of retirement, then, by all accounts, they are ready. They truly do not have enough, which is very sad.

Let me give you an example. A couple nearing retirement came to see me. At the time of our meeting Tony was sixty-two years of age and Melanie was fifty-two. Tony had embraced the idea that he would retire at sixty-five, and their goal was for Melanie to retire three years after that. Because that date was just around the corner, they had decided to look a little more closely at the details. However, they had ignored the reality of the impact they had felt when the market fell in 2008 and 2009. They had lost $1,200,000 in Tony's 401(k), and they no longer had the resources or the time to wait for the market to come back, which is what their accumulation specialist kept preaching they should do. In addition, they had no pension to rely on. If Tony were to go ahead and retire when he had planned to, the couple would run through the remainder of their life savings within five years. Yet, they only put a pencil to paper to figure these details out when Tony turned sixty-two.

I have to tell you, Tony and Melanie got so angry with me that you would have thought I was withholding a treasure map of the Sierra Madre. That happens, and I do understand. Sometimes hearing the truth, plain and simple, can hurt.

So what did I tell them?

I said, "Well, I could tell you what you want to hear. I could tell you that I am going to be like Houdini and double and triple your money, which would be a lie. Alternatively, I could show you what the figures are, and you could make some logical choices and still salvage your retirement."

The bottom line was that Tony could not realistically retire until age sixty-six. Even then, while his wife remained young, he would have to continue to work part-time until at least seventy, if his health allowed it. Melanie would also have to work at least part-time until she was sixty or sixty-two. We crunched the numbers and were able to make the figures work with these adjustments. We even brainstormed some home business ideas, such as a pet-walking or errand-running service, as alternative options for income.

Here is another example of conventional wisdom from the good old days, which you may have to reconsider today. It is a great feeling to have your house paid off, and if you can accomplish that prior

THE THREE FINANCIAL PHASES

to or just at retirement, that is terrific. Doing so means one less bill you will have in retirement. However, much of the time, I have seen people take what little they have accumulated, cash out, and pay off a house. That can be a huge disadvantage, because at that point the money is sitting in the walls of the house; it cannot be used to provide an income stream.

I recently spoke with a couple who were within seven years of retirement. Their plan was to cash out their 401(k) when they retired and use it to pay off their house. The way they saw it, their monthly $1,000 house payment would go away, and they would have a solid roof over their heads.

I told them, "I am not one of those people who will recommend that you never pay off your house because you are going to lose the write-off, or one who would say you should take the money and put it in the market instead of paying off the house. I do not believe in risking that. However, if you have not gotten it paid off by the time you are within five or ten years of retirement and you do not have a sizeable nest egg, you probably do not want to cash out those accounts in order to pay off your house, since you may never be able to replenish them."

Worse yet, the couple wanted to cash out a 401(k) that was entirely taxable. Cashing out meant they would lose more than 28 percent to the tax man and have very few reserves left. They just had not thought through the ramifications of such a decision. Having the right advisor by your side for these decisions can save you from making costly miscalculations.

Another threat to your retirement is the very real possibility of a catastrophic illness. Even if you are confident that such a thing will never happen to you, you need to craft a plan that protects your nest egg from financial devastation and saves your loved ones from having to go into crisis-planning mode when they are already trying to cope emotionally with an unexpected blow. Unfortunately, I could fill this book with sad stories of people who did not plan for such eventualities, because they believed events like that were never going to happen to them. Let me let you in on the good news: There are many simple, creative strategies you can implement so that you do not become one of those sad stories. I discuss them in Chapter Four.

Again, the action you need to take during the preservation phase is geared to keeping your money safe, not doubling or tripling it, and to do this you have to know how much of that money you need to protect. **You cannot afford to risk what you cannot afford to lose.** This bottom-line number will drive all your plans at this stage, so it is critical to calculate that number carefully. You have to determine how much dependable income you need coming in each month to support the wants and needs of you and your spouse, while also planning for the possibility that one spouse may predecease the other. You may not get to jump off a bridge together, holding hands, as my husband promised me we would do. Having a solid income-planning strategy in place will cover you both for that almost-certain eventuality.

Every day, I encounter people who really do not paint a detailed picture of what they want their retirement to look like. They act much more like Van Gogh than Michelangelo. They do not make a budget, they do not do the necessary planning, and they do not consider all risks. Often, even very smart people have no idea what they spend. For example, a couple who came in to see me together made about $150,000 per year. Of that $150,000, they were giving Uncle Sam about $25,000 in taxes and saving about $10,000 a year. When I asked them what their monthly cost of living was, they told me that they were spending $6,000 a month on everything. I looked at them and said, "Well, where's the other $43,000?" They did not have an answer for me.

Too often, what I find is that people are not conscious of their spending habits, and they are not zeroed in on precisely what it takes to finance their lifestyle. When they arrive at my office and we paint a scene of their idyllic retirement, they will throw out ideas such as "We only need half of what we are living on now. We'll be simpler people without that daily commute, those dress clothes, or that latte." However, when we apply more brushstrokes to depict the dollars and cents required to cover basic needs and definite wants, the dollar figure that emerges seems more like an image in a Salvador Dali piece: it is surreal and jarring to every sense of security they had about their retired life up to that point. Rude as it may be, this is a necessary awakening.

Most people assume they are going to spend much less in retirement. But do they? In a word, no. The least that I have ever seen anyone shave expenses in retirement was by moving down to 80 percent of the expenses of their working years. Generally, people spend at least as much when they are retired, if not more. Think about it: as a retiree, you have more time to spend, sprucing up the house, traveling, or shopping for the grandkids. With proper planning and proper allocation of your funds, you should be able to do all of that. Yet I still see many people who have saved a great deal of money but do not understand that if they just put that money in the right places, thereby creating income streams, instead of trying to double or triple their money, they could finance a great retirement.

PHASE III: THE DISTRIBUTION STAGE: WHO GETS YOUR MONEY SHOULD BE YOUR CHOICE

The final financial phase is the **distribution phase.** In this phase, you make determinations about and plans for how and to whom you will distribute all assets of your estate. When I work with clients, we develop a distribution plan in tandem with preservation planning, a process that has no adverse effects on my clients' lifestyle in retirement. I design both plans simultaneously to ensure that the clients' hard-earned, accumulated money, which we are carefully preserving, becomes a legacy of love instead of a potential tax bomb. Once again, the best form of prevention is a comprehensive and, in this case, integrated plan.

There are serious consequences to having a poorly developed distribution plan. If you have not planned properly—say, for example, you failed to set up a trust—it is possible everything you own could go to probate. Probate is a time-consuming and expensive process. While every state has different probate regulations, generally each set of regulations involves extensive fees and cumbersome procedures. During probate, some administrator your family has never met is going to come in and put a price on all of your possessions. This is a public process, which means that everybody and anybody can find out what you have left behind, to whom you owed money, and to whom you left what. The probate process also leaves things open for anybody to come along and contest the decisions. If you have a large estate, things become even worse, since your heirs could end up paying federal estate tax as well. A perfect example of an estate fiasco is that of Howard Hughes. He died without even leaving a will, let alone a trust, and it took thirty-four years for his estate to finally be settled. I find unfathomable the amount of dollars lost to taxes because of his failure to set things up properly. I could write an entire additional book of stories about people with defunct estate plans. Such occurrences are so unnecessary. A properly set-up estate plan assures you that your designated beneficiaries and heirs do not have to engage in complicated, draining, legal procedures in order to claim your intended legacy. These plans are not hard to set up and are worth the time to do.

Retirement accounts are an entirely different issue. If they are not structured properly, all of your pretax money comes out at once. It could suddenly propel your beneficiaries into the highest possible tax bracket. I have seen retirement accounts that were so shoddily structured that 70 percent of the account eventually went to taxes. If you have a carefully designed plan, you can take that same account and triple or quadruple it by making it into an inherited IRA, thereby bestowing a comfortable legacy. We will get into that in a subsequent chapter.

The point I am trying to make here is that if you do not do proper planning, you will encounter numerous pitfalls with irrevocable consequences. You can easily avoid all of them if you and your advisors have identified and implemented the appropriate strategies. Now that I have said that, turn the page. Let's roll up our sleeves and get started.

TAXING TIMES

Do Not Pay More than Your Fair Share

TAXING TIMES

Do Not Pay More than Your Fair Share

Dear IRS, I am writing to you to cancel my subscription. Please remove my name from your mailing list.

—CHARLES M. SCHULZ

If only our taxes could be as easily dispensed with as a letter to the IRS. Sorry, Charlie Brown, that football will always be taken away before you can kick it. We cannot control what our government is going to do in regard to taxes, even by making a polite request. If you take into consideration the facts that interest rates are at a historic low and that our country's debt has already gone through the roof (and is fast approaching the stratosphere), I think it is safe to say that taxes are going to go up. So, can we do anything to protect ourselves from the uncertainty of how high and therefore how much we will pay? Of course we can. The key is to be proactive, rather than reactive. Something we need to understand is that there is a direct correlation between where we invest our money, how we withdraw it, and the amount of tax we pay. It does no good to get hung up on, or scream and carry on about, the tax rate. We need to get over ourselves and, instead, focus on what aspects of taxation we can control, which in this case is where we put the money and how we take it out.

Many people do not have a tax plan that is strategically coordinated with an investment portfolio to align with and leverage unique regulations—and sometimes loopholes—to one advantage: the investor's. Do you know why? The answer is because many people trust that their accountant will do that for them. Therefore, they do not concern themselves with it or ask any questions about it. (Please know that I am not disrespecting any accountants out there.) Nine times out of ten this is just plain wrong. Your accountant's role is to review what you have already done and, based on those results, navigate through the myriad of ever-changing tax laws to tell you what you owe, keep you compliant, and make sure that you pay no more than your fair share of taxes within the confines of the law. That is your accountant's job. End of story. Do not get me wrong here. I do not mean to suggest that this is not important. However, I want to emphasize that if you want to take control of what you pay in taxes, you must have an overall coordinated plan. That plan must take into account where you put your money and the type of tax status that this money has (pretax, after-tax, tax-free, etc.) while you are accumulating it, as well as how you will withdraw the money later, in coordination with your overall investment strategy. While an accountant does not usually do this with you, the right retirement planning advisor will.

How do you know if you are with the right advisor? The means by which you find out is quite simple. Ask yourself, is your advisor looking at your tax return, making recommendations as to where you should be investing your money, and explaining the tax ramifications of those suggestions? Every day at my company we review people's tax returns, and usually we are able to suggest some strategy to reduce or eliminate some tax dollars. Sometimes it is only a little bit, but often it is significant.

Let me give you an example. One day, Joe and Ida came to see me. Joe was sixty-four years old and Ida was sixty-two, and both had just retired. Joe had worked thirty years as an engineer at the same company, which is unusual today, and Ida had worked part-time for the previous ten years. Prior to that, she had worked full-time in their home, raising their four children. They were conservative, hard-working, and thrifty people who had managed to save $150,000 in Ida's IRA, $625,000 in Joe's 401(k), and $550,000 in CDs. They had no debts, not even a mortgage. Joe had a pension, and they both had just applied for Social Security. Their accountant had been with them for eighteen years and they loved him because, as they said, they had never had a bit of trouble from the IRS. They had had the same financial advisor for more than fifteen years, and they described him as a good guy who gave great Christmas parties each year. When the market went down in 2008, they lost only half as much as their friends had lost. Wow! Between their accountant and their advisor, Joe and Ida were set—right? Unfortunately, they were not.

Bear in mind that Joe and Ida had only come to see me because they wanted to learn more about a multigenerational IRA. As far as they were concerned, they were in great shape. However, after the first few minutes of our meeting, I discovered that their accountant and advisor never communicated. Joe and Ida were making their own decisions about from where to take income. They were following the conventional wisdom their advisor preached, which was, "Do not touch your 401(k) and IRA money until the government requires you to do so at age seventy-and-one-half." They were both taking their Social Security because they wanted to make sure they received the money before Social Security went broke. As smart as Ida and

Joe had been about saving and becoming debt-free, as smart as their accountant was about making sure that they did not get entangled with the IRS, and as ably as their advisor had helped them to grow their money, they still did not have a well-coordinated retirement plan.

To begin with, by looking quickly through their tax returns, I showed them how they could save $1,400 a year in taxes just by repositioning some of their taxable CD money to short term tax-free municipal bonds. I clearly showed them the impact of this by pulling up their tax return and creating a side-by-side revised return. This is just a simple example of the degree to which you can control what you pay in taxes.

In my thirty-plus years in the industry I have taken many, many educational courses. Of all of them, the one that has probably been the most beneficial to my clients is the ongoing mentoring I receive on intensive and extensive levels as a charter member of the prestigious Master Elite IRA group run by Ed Slott, the foremost authority on IRA tax planning and distribution planning. If you do not know who Ed is, I recommend you go to his website (www.irahelp.com). You can also check your local PBS television station for **Ed Slott's Retirement Rescue!,** a powerful call-to-action television program for American consumers concerned about their retirement.

> *For information on IRA tax and distribution planning, check out Ed Slott's website: www.irahelp.com or listen to his television program,* **Retirement Rescue!,** *on your local PBS television station*

Why has this education been so invaluable? Think about this for a moment. If you are like most people, you have followed the conventional wisdom of saving as much as you could in a tax-deferred account—an IRA, 401(k), and so forth—because of the idea that you remain in a higher tax bracket while you are working than the bracket you will be in when you retire and lose your paycheck. That makes perfect sense, right?

Well, let's think about that. When IRAs first came out this was true—look at the tax rates—but times have changed. While tax rates are currently at a historic low, we can reasonably assume taxes are going up. For this and many more reasons, many people find when they retire that they are, in fact, not going to be in a lower bracket. Instead, they are in the same bracket and probably will be in a higher one in the future.

Year	Top Federal Income Tax Rate
2011	35%
2003-2010	35%
2002	38.6%
2001	39.1%
1993-2000	39.6%
1991-1992	31%
1988-1990	28%
1987	38.5%
1982-1986	50%
1965-1981	70%
1964	77%
1954-1963	91%
1952-1953	92%
1946-1951	91%
1944-1945	94%

Yet, most people leave the majority of their retirement nest egg in pretax accounts, which means that every dollar that comes out will be taxed.

If you do not plan strategically, you may be setting up a "tax bomb" for yourself and your heirs.

Inside these retirement accounts are all kinds of crazy rules and regulations that could lead to more complications and taxes when you touch the money if they are not handled properly. Take

the process of rolling over your 401(k) to an IRA. There are multiple ways to mess that up and trigger a tax bomb. For example, suppose an individual is in collective receipt of his/her 401(k) money because he/she has left a company or retired. If the 401(k) money is made out to him/her instead of going directly to another trustee, and if for any reason the account holder does not get the money back into a retirement-type account within sixty days, then boom! It all becomes taxable. If you think this type of thing simply does not happen, think again. It happens far more often than you think. That is why working with the right advisor, preferably someone who has expertise in this area, is imperative. This will save you from unnecessary tax implications.

If you inherit an IRA and it is managed incorrectly, Uncle Sam can take up to 70 percent of that money in unnecessary taxes. Let me give you a perfect example. I have a client who inherited her father's rather large IRA, which resided with a bank.[7] To make a long story short, the bank employees had convinced my client that she could add her father's IRA to her own IRA account, which my firm handled. The bank employees were simply going to send the check and be done with the transaction. If they had done so, not only would every last dollar of this $2 million IRA have become taxable, it would have also cost my client an additional 6 percent penalty, since she would have overfunded her IRA. Thank goodness she knew that this transaction fell into my area of expertise, so she came in to meet with me to make sure the bank employees were processing the paperwork correctly. Because of that, we successfully avoided a huge tax bomb. This is one area in which it is crucial to work with a specialist. The right specialist who knows how to handle such accounts correctly

---

7   On a side note, banks and wire houses are probably the worst custodians of IRA accounts if you want to pass on generational wealth. These institutions are not set up or structured to handle this type of account, and their representatives really do not understand the fine points.

will ensure that those same tax bombs are turned into generational wealth and legacies of love.

My extensive education in this area has given me the knowledge and ability to help many people handle their accounts in the most tax advantageous way. Truly, at my firm we have saved our clients from paying tremendous tax dollars and enabled them to pass on more of their wealth to future generations. As complicated as this stuff can be, the government has established many loopholes, if you know where to look, that can save you and your heirs significant funds. If you use them correctly, you can take advantage of the Roth IRA, the Roth 401(k), or the Roth conversion, all of which are inherently capable of maximizing your money. This gift from Uncle Sam is far too often left on the table.

Farmers have a saying: "I would rather pay tax on my seed than on the harvest."

Why? The answer is they have less seed than harvest, so there will be less tax to pay.

Let's equate that to the IRA and the Roth for a moment. An IRA, or 401(k), is an account in which you put your money to grow before you pay tax on it. The money grows tax-deferred until you take it out. The government requires you to begin withdrawing it at age seventy-and-one-half, essentially taxing the harvest rather than the seed, which is a big "gotcha." Another sneaky "gotcha" hits if your kids inherit this IRA money: if they take all the

money out at once, and most do, they will pay taxes on the entire amount. Fortunately, there are strategies you can employ to prevent this, which I will discuss later on in this chapter.

If you use a Roth IRA or a Roth 401(k), you pay taxes on the money before you put it into the account. Then it grows, tax-free, forever. As an additional benefit, you will not pay taxes when you take it out, and your heirs will not have to pay taxes either. Thus, you pay the tax on the seed, not the harvest. That is a huge advantage that many miss because they are not thinking of long-term impacts. However, it is never too late to change your strategy. The government permits you to convert your pretax accounts, such as IRAs, to tax-free Roth accounts at any time. You just have to be prepared to pay the taxes right then.

It seems this is where most people stop and think, "Why would I do that?" Well, work with me here. If taxes are going up, why would you not take advantage of paying now to save more over the long haul? Furthermore, nothing forces you to convert all your pretax accounts to tax-free ones at once. With regard to our clients, we strategically implement this as Roth rollouts each year. That way, we keep them in the same tax bracket and immediately get their money growing tax-free. If you do not know about Roth rollouts, you are missing the boat. They are simple conversions of pretax funds to tax-free money that you can enact without raising your tax bracket one penny.

Another beneficial strategy which we implement into our clients' distribution plans is the multigenerational IRA, also known as a stretch IRA. While most people have never heard of this opportunity, it is clearly described in the IRS *Publication 590*, that authoritative guide to understanding all things related to your individual retirement arrangements.

What can a multigenerational IRA do for you? If you have an IRA, a 401(k), or any type of pretax retirement account, when you die, your surviving spouse can transfer your retirement account to his or her own IRA without paying taxes on it until he or she draws the money out. However, when the only surviving spouse dies, if

his or her heirs inherit the account, they cannot add it to their own account. If they do, they have to pay taxes on every dollar of the account right then and there. In addition, they are hit with a penalty for overfunding the account. Ouch!

Let me put this in perspective for you. You work your entire life and accumulate an IRA. Let's say it is worth $500,000 when your kids inherit it. If they take that money out or add it to their own IRAs, every dollar will be taxed from a range of 30 to 70 percent, depending on specifics. That means that $150,000 to $350,000 will go to Uncle Sam. However, if the account is handled properly, this does not have to happen; it is a travesty of justice if this high taxation occurs.

Fortunately, under Code 529, the IRS allows you to set up a multigenerational IRA for free. That means that when you die, a properly titled, inherited IRA is passed on to your heirs. Instead of having to pay taxes on that lump sum, they can wait as it grows in deferral for generations. They only pay taxes on the amounts that they are required to take out in minimum distributions. Ergo, you have created generational wealth. According to Ed Slott, a properly constructed, multigenerational IRA, depending on specifics, could exist for more than one hundred years. That's what I am talking about!

Let me be clear. **Without changing your retirement account in terms of benefits and your ability to access it during your lifetime, you can properly set up an account as a multigenerational IRA that will create a legacy of love, not a tax bomb.** Thanks to this knowledge, my team and I are doing this every day in our practice. There is absolutely no reason to throw your wealth away.

If you have a retirement account, go to www.irahelp.com. Watch Ed's video in which he addresses the fact that most advisors do not set up a multigenerational IRA account properly. If you have a retirement account and want to make sure that it is handled correctly in your lifetime and for your heirs, make sure your advisor is an expert in this area.

How can you know whether or not the advisor with whom you are considering working is, in fact, an expert?

Here are some questions you will want to ask him or her before making your choice:

1. I know this area requires specialized knowledge in IRA distribution planning.
   Do you have expertise in this area?
   How would I know that?

2. What books have you read on the topic? (You should actually look at the books in the advisor's office. If the

binding cracks when you open them, run; that's the first time that book was ever opened.)

3. What professional training do you currently take in IRA distribution planning?

   What courses or programs have you taken?

   Can you show me the last course manual you received?

4. How do you stay up to date on key IRA tax laws?

   What services or resources do you rely on to stay current?

   Can you show me a sample?

5. What is the latest IRA tax rule you are aware of?

   When did it occur?

6. How do you determine the best option for my lump sum distribution?

   What are all of my choices?

7. How would you keep track of my IRA beneficiary form?

   When should I update my IRA beneficiary form?

   What are the key events that would trigger a need for a review?

8. Can you show me the IRS life expectancy tables?

9. Do you know what will happen to my IRA after I die?

   How will you make sure that my beneficiary will get the stretch IRA?

10. To whom do you turn when you have questions on IRA distribution planning?

(This question is important, because nobody can know it all.)

The bottom line is that when it comes to taxes, do not assume your accountant is doing what needs to be done to reduce and eliminate your taxes. Instead, be proactive and be sure that your investments are invested properly, not only in terms of return but also in terms of tax efficiency. Furthermore, make sure that you have a well-laid-out plan for how to accumulate wealth in a tax-advantageous manner, as well as how to safely withdraw that money in retirement. If you follow some simple steps as part of a coordinated plan, you will find these goals are not hard to achieve.

Again, the point to remember here is that there are some things you can control and need to control, and taxes are certainly among those things. You need to make certain that your advisor is working with you to ensure that he or she is saving you money both now and down the line.

CATASTROPHIC ILLNESS

Hope for the Best; Plan for the Worst

CATASTROPHIC ILLNESS

Hope for the Best; Plan for the Worst

Catastrophic illness is probably my least favorite topic. However, as uncomfortable as the subject is, it would be irresponsible of me not to bring it up.

Catastrophic illness can strike anyone at any time. Although we can implement preventive health measures, such as exercise and healthy eating, we cannot anticipate what unexpected health challenges we will face as we age. A debilitating accident, a cancer diagnosis, or the onset of a disease such as Alzheimer's can occur with little notice. Once one of these events takes place, it can consume nearly all of your and your family's attention as you work to find the best immediate treatments. Ultimately, the knowledge of who among us will eventually need custodial care is held in the hands of higher powers. What we hold is the power to protect our loved ones and ourselves from the financial consequences of a major illness or injury.

Nobody wants to think about having a catastrophic illness, because they think it is "not going to happen to" them. Many people prefer to sweep any thought of illness under the carpet; they neglect to discuss it as part of their retirement planning. However, the fact of the matter is that such catastrophes happen to many people. As

I explained at the beginning of this book, the good news is that we are living longer, and the bad news is that we are living longer. As lifespans extend, more and more people have a need for some type of custodial care. For many very good reasons, creating a retirement plan that takes into account the possibility of a catastrophic illness and the accompanying health-care costs is practicing good medicine, being fiscally responsible, and performing a true act of loving kindness to your family.

> *About 70 percent of people over the age of sixty-five will require long-term-care services, including using assisted living, staying at a nursing home, or receiving home care. Costs for such services, on average, range from $4,000 to $8,000 per month.*
>
> *According to U.S. Department of Health and Human Services*

The number-one reason for making such a plan is that a catastrophic illness suffered by you or your spouse could be financially devastating for your loved ones. According to the U.S. Department of Health and Human Services, at some point, about 70 percent of people over the age of sixty-five will require long-term-care services, including using assisted living, staying at a nursing home, or receiving home care. Costs for such services, on average, range from $4,000 to $8,000 per month. The number-two reason is to protect yourself. If you do not have enough money to pay for care, you could end up in a situation in which the quality of your care is at risk. It is already emotionally wrenching to watch a loved one suffer. However, it is even more devastating if family members cannot afford to give their loved one the required type of care. These are two very good reasons for ensuring that your family is protected from both of these possibilities.

When I talk about a catastrophic illness as something that is extremely costly, most people are puzzled. Puzzlement is a very common reaction at the educational workshops my firm runs to help people become informed about this topic. When clients come in, they will say things to me such as, "I know that health care is very expensive today, Phillis, but I have Medicare and I've got a great Medicare supplement. If I need something, I am going to be fairly well protected." Well, if a client needs an operation, or has an illness that requires medical attention, this statement is right. The client will not have much out-of-pocket expense, even for something as major as a heart transplant. For the most part, each of them is going to be covered.

However, the type of catastrophic illness I am concerned with here—whether it is the result of an accident or dementia—is one that would cause someone to need help with the basic activities of daily living, such as feeding themselves, moving in and out of chairs, taking medications, and so forth. People do not realize that the government does not pay for that kind of care under Medicare, and no Medicare supplement covers such an eventuality. At best, Medicare and the Medicare supplement will cover the first ninety days of custodial care if those days are related to a hospital stay. That type of custodial care, whether it is offered at home, at an assisted living facility, or at a nursing home, is extremely expensive. Its cost could well exceed $60,000 to $100,000 per year. Additionally, according to AARP, once people reach the age of sixty-five, there is a 70 percent chance that one out of two will spend time in a nursing home facility, with the average stay lasting about 2.9 years. These numbers cannot be ignored.

You have to have a plan, as the chart I have included below demonstrates, because these astronomical nursing home costs are only going to go up.

2010 Average Nursing Home & Assisted Living Costs Per State

State	NH Cost	AL Cost	State	NH Cost	AL Cost	State	NH Cost	AL Cost
AL	$ 5,310	$ 2,579	ME	$ 8,190	$ 4,575	PA	$ 7,740	$ 3,328
AK	$ 20,610	$ 4,372	MD	$ 7,680	$ 4,092	RI	$ 8,370	$ 3,440
AZ	$ 7,050	$ 2,998	MA	$ 9,870	$ 4,468	SC	$ 5,730	$ 3,063
AR	$ 4,650	$ 2,170	MI	$ 6,600	$ 3,088	SD	$ 5,400	$ 2,520
CA	$ 8,610	$ 3,601	MN	$ 462	$ 2,961	TN	$ 5,700	$ 3,216
CO	$ 6,630	$ 3,069	MS	$ 5,760	$ 2,466	TX	$ 5,490	$ 3,091
CT	$ 11,280	$ 4,622	MO	$ 4,710	$ 2,948	UT	$ 5,850	$ 2,776
DC	$ 8,700	$ 5,231	MT	$ 5,490	$ 2,709	VT	$ 7,830	$ 4,627
DE	$ 7,710	$ 4,608	NE	$ 5,100	$ 2,714	VA	$ 6,360	$ 3,743
FL	$ 7,260	$ 2,996	NV	$ 7,200	$ 3,140	WA	$ 7,590	$ 2,979
GA	$ 5,310	$ 3,116	NH	$ 8,790	$ 4,068	WV	$ 6,420	$ 3,242
HI	$ 10,920	$ 4,223	NJ	$ 9,210	$ 4,286	WI	$ 7,200	$ 3,375
ID	$ 6,840	$ 2,985	NM	$ 6,420	$ 2,685	WY	$ 6,090	$ 2,909
IL	$ 6,480	$ 3,451	NY	$ 10,500	$ 3,701			
IN	$ 6,510	$ 2,799	NC	$ 6,120	$ 3,397	National Averages		
IA	$ 4,770	$ 2,681	ND	$ 4,920	$ 2,408	Nursing Home		$ 6,870
KS	$ 4,740	$ 3,214	OH	$ 6,540	$ 3,199	Assisted Living		$ 3,293
KY	$ 6,180	$ 2,931	OK	$ 5,400	$ 2,628			
LA	$ 4,230	$ 2,512	OR	$ 7,380	$ 3,120			

Another myth that quickly needs to be dispelled is that it is easy to qualify for Medicaid. People think, "Oh, I'll just spend all my money or hide all my money. Then I'll qualify for Medicaid, and Medicaid will take care of me. After all, I've paid into the system all these years." Well, it is true that it used to be fairly easy to give away your assets right before you went into a nursing home and then have Medicaid cover you. Today, doing so is a very difficult task. Previously, all long-term-care beds and Medicaid facilities were the same, whether the facility received Medicaid or private payments.

As an example of this change in the Medicaid situation, my father-in-law, a very proud man, paid for nursing home care for five years himself, while the gentleman in the very next bed received the very same care courtesy of Medicaid. This was several years ago. Today, it is all totally different. First of all, the government is practically broke, so qualifying for Medicaid is not easy. You have to be indigent. If you have a spouse, you have to leave that spouse at home with very few assets and a black cloud hanging over his or her head before Medicaid will step in and pay for this type of care.

There is only one other way you can qualify for Medicaid, and that is by giving all of your assets away, perhaps to your children, or by putting your money in an irrevocable trust to which you have no access, and you must give away your money or complete this trust five years and one minute before you ever need that type of care. This scenario is very problematic because you lose control of your money. What's more, if your children are married and one of them divorces, half of that money becomes your ex-in-law's. If one of your kids loses a lawsuit, what was your money goes to paying that off. Beating the system this way is not as easy as it looks.

Secondly, the type of facility Medicaid pays for is not the type that the average person would ever want to be in, unless he or she has absolutely no choice. People do not believe this until they see these facilities for themselves. For that matter, even the facility that Medicare covers is probably one to which you would not want to be admitted.

The real point I'm making here is that a health-care crisis may well be in your future, and it is not Uncle Sam who will be paying for it!

There are various methods you can use to protect yourself from the nursing home dilemma. Many people think that long-term-care insurance is their only option, but you have other choices, and you must have a plan. The consequences of not planning are both financially and emotionally devastating. This topic matters to me for personal reasons, and I would like to share a story that underscores why I am so passionate about it. From my heart to your heart, I hope this story resonates and saves you some of the pain that I have seen and personally experienced.

Earlier in this book I described the story of my dad dying in an automobile accident. My mom, who was just fifty-nine years old at that time, was young, healthy, and vibrant. At that point, even though I had been a financial planner for many years and was taking good care of her money, I was in denial, like everybody else, about the possibility that my mom would ever need any type of custodial care. The year after my dad died, when she asked me to write her long-term-care insurance, I said, "What are you talking about? That's not going to happen." However, she insisted, so I reluctantly did it, knowing deep down it was the right thing to do. In the back of my mind, I always thought that if that situation came to be, we would only use the home-health-care benefit on that policy. God forbid she would ever need that type of care. Given my work responsibilities, I imagined that we would have someone come into the home and take care of her, and I convinced myself that she would never need to go into a facility.

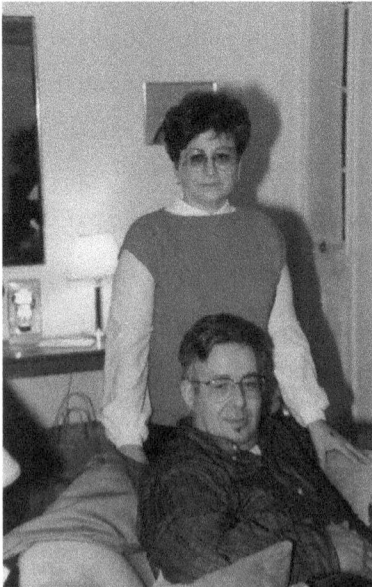

My mom took out this policy when she was sixty years old. She was a healthy seventy-three-year-old woman when she went on a cruise with her friends. On their drive home from California to Arizona they were in a terrible automobile accident. My mom was thrown a hundred feet from the car and sustained multiple injuries, including a traumatic head injury. Because she was healthy, she pulled through. She came out of her coma, and even though her body had been terribly beaten up, she recovered. Yet, the very day she was as healed from the accident as she could be, the doctors wanted her out of the hospital.

Unfortunately, at that point in time, I had to come to terms with the fact that her overall physical health was still a challenge; bringing her home was not yet an option. We had set up my home with a separate grandmother's wing, much like the one we used to tease her about before her accident. My husband, who had a great relationship with my mom, was ready to be an attentive companion, and my children were looking forward to pampering her, but my mom's condition would not allow her to return to our home for the next phase of her convalescence. We had to start looking for a nursing home.

I had watched my mother suffer, day in and day out, for more than three months, and the last thing I wanted to do was relocate her to a cold, sterile, stranger-filled facility with overworked and underpaid staff. Obviously, her physical outcome was in God's hands. Fortunately, because we had done the planning—establishing long-term-care insurance as well as putting her money in a safe account where it was earning a steady, reliable stream of income—she could be assured of access to quality services. We started by visiting the facilities that Medicare would cover for the first ninety or one hundred days, but they were grossly inadequate and depressing. We knew these environments would drastically impede Mom's recovery. Instead, we found a better fit for her: a private nursing-home facility, the best that we could find. Because of the planning we had done, we did not have to worry. The money was there. Unfortunately, my mom's situation deteriorated due to the onset of a previously undetected cancer. Eventually, she required the retention of a nurse's aide in addition to my family's constant care and visits. Nine months to the day of the accident, my mom passed away. It was the most horrible nine months in my life. Worrying about her kept me up nights, and I have not been the same since. The only silver lining in this catastrophe, the one comfort that kept me from totally losing it, was that we were able to give her the best possible type of surroundings, medical care, and nursing services that money could buy.

I loved my mom dearly, and I know there are many kids out there who love their parents as much as my brother and I loved our mom and dad. We were fortunate that we had made plans that provided excellent care for our mom, but experiencing this situation made me think about other people. What if they could not afford that level of care? What if my dad had been alive and had had to put my mom in a home but could not afford to do so? Emotionally, that would push anybody over the edge. Having gone through this type of experience, I can tell you that it is something to avoid at all costs, and you can avoid it with good planning. My mom and dad were average people. After Dad died, Mom did not have a lot of money, but she did have the foresight and willingness to invest in this type of protection. With the right plan, everyone can protect what they have and be assured that if the worst does happen, the best quality of care that they or a family member needs, can be arranged.

Please do not be in denial. Set up a plan so that, God forbid, the people you love not only don't have to watch you suffer, but don't have to watch you suffer in miserable conditions. Most people today would have to struggle to afford quality care for parents who had not planned for this. You do not want to leave that burden on your loved ones' shoulders.

Long-term-care insurance is not the only option you have with which to provide financial protection in the event of a catastrophic illness. I understand that many people do not purchase long-term-care insurance because it is another bill for services that, in their hearts, they do not believe they will ever need to use. If they do not use it, they are going to lose the money spent to buy it. I agree with them. After all, long-term-care insurance is probably not my first choice, especially today, given that the premiums are all experience rated, just like auto and homeowners' insurance. If the insurer's experience is unfavorable and the company starts losing money, premiums can increase. This increase typically happens when you are older, are on a fixed income, and are approaching the age at which the need for long-term care is a real risk factor. This means the premium you take on today can increase later, which I see happen to clients all the time. Do not get me wrong. If you already have long-term-care insurance, or you can afford it and qualify for it medically, do not cancel it or reject it based upon what I have said. Just be prudent.

In other words, if you do have this insurance, make sure you have a customized, well-thought-out set of benefits for that type of insurance. Keep it lean and mean; you probably do not need to have full coverage for every contingency. Do not get stuck with a great deal of expensive, worthless bells and whistles in your contract. I see too many people who have been sold a bill of goods by a long-term-care salesperson, and they have all these extras they are paying for that are effectively meaningless in terms of what the policy will do for them. The only parties who benefit from that type of a contract are the people who sold it to you, in terms of the commission, and, of course, the insurance company.

If you have long-term-care insurance, make sure that you understand each benefit; if you cannot understand it and your salesperson cannot make it clear to you, there is no reason to have it. In addition, make sure that the costs that you could pay from interest on investments or pensions, which you are not tapping into, are not things you are paying for on your policy.

Fortunately, there are other creative options for long-term care that you are likely to find more palatable. Today, companies link long-term-care benefits to life insurance products and annuity products. In 2006, when the Pension Protection Act came out with benefits, the government made significant changes in the taxation of those riders attached to insurance and annuity products. What that means is that there are other avenues for people to explore that do not have the downside of losing it if you do not use it. If you have life insurance with a long-term-care benefit attached, even if you never need that long-term care, the life insurance will ultimately pay off to your beneficiary, so it is not lost. If you have an annuity with a long-term-care

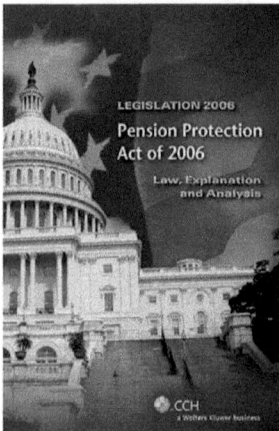

benefit attached, the annuity is still an investment that can give you supplemental lifetime income and, if you need it, long-term care.

About two years ago, a couple came into my office. They seemed to have everything set for their income needs in retirement, and they were comfortable in their investments. However, they had no plan to accommodate a catastrophic illness. Unfortunately, the wife had recently been diagnosed with multiple sclerosis (MS). When you suddenly discover you may need long-term-care insurance, you can get it—right? Wrong. You have to be able to qualify medically. However, due to the Pension Protection Act of 2006, the government has recently offered people a great deal of flexibility through asset-based insurance. So, without any evidence of insurability, I set up an annuity for this couple that carried a long-term-care rider. This meant that their income would double if and when the wife needed care. Inevitably, my client's MS progressed. Yet, because of proper planning, she and her husband were able to protect the rest of their estate from costly out-of-pocket medical expenses. Instead, they used the long-term-care income doubler.

When conducting proper retirement planning, you must lay everything out, including a plan to address a health-care crisis. Simply ignoring the topic is not a realistic option. Always plan for the worst and hope for the best. It is incredibly important to protect the retirement of which you have both dreamed and rightfully earned through your hard work and saving.

With the right set of circumstances, these newer insurance options can provide people with creative strategies that let them kill two birds with one stone. I meet many people who recognize that, perhaps, they could eventually endure a catastrophic illness situation, but they do not want to go the traditional long-term-care insurance route because of the use-it-or-lose-it issue and because of the fact that rates can and do go up. Instead, these individuals are completely self-insuring. I see their point. What I want people to know is that if you incorporate the new, aggressive types of products into your financial planning, you can use other people's money and leverage your own money while doing so.

For example, I recently met with Lorraine, a sixty-five-year-old woman, who said to me, "Phillis, I recognize having a health-care crisis could be a costly issue, so I've put $100,000 of my portfolio aside. I am earning interest on it. I will not touch it. That will be my long-term-care money." I showed her how to move that investment from the left hand to the right hand by putting it into benefit-linked life insurance. That is what I refer to as the "three-bucket approach." Using this approach, Lorraine could take that $100,000 inside this life insurance product and place it in the first bucket, where she could have it create a benefit of five times that amount for any type of long-term-care needs she might have, whether relating to home health, assisted living, or nursing home care.

Lorraine then said, "That leverage is great, Phillis, but I'd like to have my $100,000 liquid so I could take it out at any point." Well, the second bucket allows her to have total liquidity; she could have this money back any time she wants it.

For Lorraine, the third bucket covers the best of all possible outcomes: she does not go into a nursing home, she does not have a catastrophic illness, and she does not need her money back. When she dies, this money will be leveraged as an income-tax-free death benefit to her beneficiaries. That $100,000 for Lorraine will end up being about $166,000 as a death benefit. Do the math yourself; assuming that a 65-year-old lives 20 years, it's still a good rate of return at 3% per year, income tax-free.

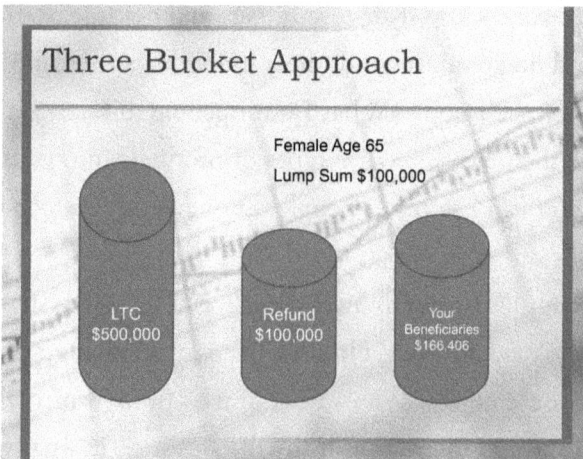

Three Bucket Approach

Female Age 65
Lump Sum $100,000

LTC
$500,000

Refund
$100,000

Your
Beneficiaries
$166,406

The above is not the only method by which you can leverage when you are self-insuring. In my practice I meet many people who have life insurance they have paid into for years and who have amassed a considerable amount of cash. In some cases, the paid-up contract is collecting dust in a drawer, and the insurance holders have forgotten they had it. Very often, I am able to work with clients to reposition those assets, tax-free, to these newer type of vehicles, thereby making better use of an existing asset to offset the potential threat of a catastrophic illness.

Another option that people can explore to cover those long-term-care costs—although, I hope, this would only be used as a last resort—is a reverse mortgage. Just to clear up any confusion, a reverse mortgage does not require you to sell your home to the government. Instead, you are loaned an amount of money based upon the value of your home, and you are never required to make a monthly payment. The accrued interest on the loan is rolled into your total mortgage balance. The house remains in your name until it is sold. When you pass away, your heirs can choose to either pay back the loan and keep the house or walk away and let the bank sell it. In either case, your family members will never personally be responsible for that debt. If you sell your home while you are living or if your heirs sell it after you die, none of you will ever be required to pay back more than the market value of the home at the time it is sold, regardless of the actual loan balance, since this is considered a nonrecourse loan. Please note I am not suggesting you pull all the equity out of your house to pay off all of your debt or go on a mad spending spree. Most people take pride in the American dream of having their homes paid off and would never consider using a home as collateral. However, if you are confronted with a catastrophic illness, and you clearly understand the ramifications of choosing a reverse mortgage, such an arrangement could work as the proverbial life raft that gets you safely to shore.

In addition, veterans and spouses of veterans have another option, which is to look at the veterans' benefits to which they or their spouses may be entitled. The wonderful Debbie Burak, who has been a guest on my radio show many times, went through an awful situation in which her parents both needed health care as a result of catastrophic events. Because of their financial situation, Debbie's parents were placed in a nursing home. Once they were there, Debbie realized that their health care was being compromised. In a state of desperation, Debbie embarked on a search for anything that could help her provide her parents with better options. Since her dad was a veteran, Debbie scoured the Veteran Administration (VA) benefit regulations until she uncovered a little-known pension that is available to anybody over the age of sixty-five who served in the US Armed Forces during wartime. Those vets, or their spouses, can collect benefits if they fit the loose definition of *disabled* according to the VA. These benefits can be as much as $1,900 a month. There is much more information available to you on Debbie's website, www. veteranaid.org. If you suspect that you may qualify for such a benefit, I urge you to investigate it.

However, I must caution you: buyer beware. Many insurance agents advertise with this benefit and use bait-and-switch techniques just to sell people financial products, so be careful. The VA prohibits anyone from charging a veteran to file a VA application. These charges are typically made by salespersons trying to sell financial products. Veterans and their spouses can only get help regarding VA matters from a veteran service organization (such as the VFW), an accredited agent, or a certified lawyer. Remember, nothing is for free. If something seems too good to be true, it probably is.

Just recently, a couple came in to meet with me regarding the situation of one of their parents. An insurance person had told them that by putting her money into an annuity inside a trust, the woman could qualify for the Veteran's Aid and Attendance Benefit, and she could use that pension money to pay for an independent living facility. Obviously, I was livid, and so were they after I explained to them that this claim was not true. Thank goodness they had turned to me before the woman made some bad financial decisions. Although I have nothing against annuities used in the right set of circumstances, in this case, they would have been used inappropriately and would have done more harm than good.

Once again, please remember that if something sounds too good to be true, you should get the facts in black and white before you act.

The consequences of a catastrophic illness can be emotionally and financially devastating. I think anyone who calls herself (or himself) an advisor but has not sat down with you and put some type of plan for such an eventuality in place is doing you a disservice. Now that you have read this section, you know the right advisor for this stage of your life will be proactive; he or she will not cause you to be reactive. I hope you realize that there are a number of different ways through which you can better prepare yourself should such an unfortunate situation present itself in your life. Remember, hope for the best, but plan for the worst.

DON'T RISK MONEY YOU CAN'T AFFORD TO LOSE

DON'T RISK MONEY YOU
CAN'T AFFORD TO LOSE

People with investments often worry about how the market is going to do. They talk about how they hope it will go up and stay up so they can afford to retire and stay retired while living a comfortable lifestyle. Some people are so concerned about this topic that after working hard their entire lives,

"Should I buy or sell?"

they retire and spend a good part of their days watching stuff such as CNBC so that how the market does basically determines how each day goes.

Does that sound familiar to you? I cannot tell you how many people have told me that if only the market had not gone down, they would be retired. Those already retired tell me that if only the market had not gone down so much, they would have been able to do such and such. They see every stock market gain as a foothold to happiness and each ascending arrow as their path to security. They hope it all will go up and stay up so they can finally stop worrying. This kind of thinking smacks of a heavy dose of "hopium," and I meet far too many people hooked on it. Using the stock market as a retirement barometer is a much more reliable indicator of how high your blood pressure will rise than how solidly your retirement dreams will play out.

Do not get me wrong. I want the market to go up too. It is nice to be in a thriving economic environment like that of the 1990s. However, the fact is that we, as average people, cannot control what the market is going to do. As quickly as it may rise, it can plummet. I say, stop wasting any more energy on wishful thinking that the market is your ticket to better retirement living. Instead, control what you can to build a dependable financial future. It is not worth being captive to the whims of a market over which you have absolutely no control and getting sick by worrying about it. Instead, call your own shots as a freethinking, savvy CEO and create a certainty in your life that assures calmness no matter what the market does. By applying a simple, tried-and-true principle of money management, which works every time, you unhitch your retirement wagon from a very fickle market and leave the stress, uncertainty, and aggravation behind you.

What is this principle? It is a simple idea: control the amount of money you put at risk in the market in the first place. All my years of experience helping people transition into retirement and navigate successfully through that retirement have taught me the importance of this one simple formula: **do not risk money that you cannot afford to lose**. In the preservation stage of your life, when time is no longer on your side and the paycheck will be disappearing imminently, do not risk money you cannot replace. Do not risk money if losing it would mean that your lifestyle would have to change. It really is that simple.

DEFINE YOUR OWN FINANCIAL DNA

This is the tough part. Really, though, it is not that tough; you just have to know your numbers. In other words, based upon your particular situation, you should know how much you can afford to lose. I think of this as defining your own financial DNA. How do you do that? Let's start with the basics. You begin by creating a vivid picture of how you want your retirement to be. Think of the activities, amenities, and components that will make it fulfilling and comfortable. Maybe you want to travel frequently. Maybe you want to help pay for your grandchildren's education. Maybe you want to golf every day or buy a new car every two years. You get the point: everyone is different. You have to lay out that lifestyle and then project a realistic budget that will support it. What does your ideal lifestyle cost?

Do you have enough saved to live the life you envision in retirement?

Once you have figured that out, determine your risk tolerance—that is, figure out how much financial and emotional risk you can take. Then, cast your eye over the time horizon and think about how long you expect to live. While this is just going to be a guesstimate, of course, you can make a fairly accurate assumption based on your health and your family's longevity. In my experience, most people plan for too short a time, so err on the side of good genes and add some years here. Next, ensure that your plan factors in both inflation and a rise in taxes. Obamacare has raised your taxes, so anticipate this type of raise in planning. Finally, your plan should include the costs of health care to cover a catastrophic illness. You know the old cliché, "Better safe than sorry." Nowhere should this be better reflected and practiced than in your retirement plan.

Next, take a look at the balance of your nest egg. Total how much you actually have saved, and then total all of your fixed sources of income: pensions, Social Security, and any other reliable, guaranteed sources of income. Through this exercise, you will see whether your vision of ideal retirement matches the reality of your numbers simply by answering some very important questions. Do you have enough saved to live the life you envision? If you do not have enough, are you willing to work longer or find ways to cut back on expenses? If you do have enough, how much of your nest egg will you need to use to maintain your lifestyle?

This may seem like a lot to tackle, but it is really pretty easy once you get going. Knowing what there is, instead of what you hope will be, puts you in control. In the back of this book, you will find a helpful budget-figuring sheet. Please use it! I see the market overwhelm so many people. They never stop to look at the reality of their own finances, so they simply do not know how much money they have to keep safe. Sadly enough, most advisors are only focused on helping clients grow their money, not on helping them design a plan to keep that money. Unfortunately, much too often I see people who do not know what the right balance between risk dollars and safety is. They keep too much in the market, and when the market inevitably goes down, so do they. That moment is when a not-so-great advisor for this stage of life tells them things such as, "Don't worry about it, the market always comes back," or "Just spend less for a while." That is ridiculous. Instead, know your number and invest accordingly.

I am proud to tell you that my clients do not succumb to either this market roller-coaster ride or the world of "hopium." I work with them to first and foremost clearly define their number and nail down how much they need to keep safe and how much they can risk. My clients know what they need to fund their lifestyle choices.

Many advisors make a big deal about diversifying a portfolio and how that will keep a client safe; they think people should separate investments into lots of bonds, lots of stocks, small-cap, mid-cap, and large-cap funds, and so on. To me, that is baloney. For someone about to retire or who is retired, the choice is simple. Diversification for that person is separated into two different worlds: the safe world, or the place you put your money that remains safe no matter what the market does, and the risk world, or the place where you take on risk that has much more of an upside potential. The safe world consists of places where you can put your money and have it guaranteed by major financial institutions such as a bank, the FDIC, the insurance companies, and the US government. Such guarantees come through fixed and fixed-index annuities, life insurance, and government bonds. The risk world, in contrast, is any other place. Below is a simple layout that should make it crystal clear:

Investments

Safe World	Risk World
Guaranteed protected from market	Not guaranteed but more potential for gain
• Savings Accounts	
• CD's	• Stocks
• Money Market	• Bonds
• Cash Value Life Insurance	• Mutual Funds
• Fixed/Fixed Index Annuities	• ETF's
• Government Bonds	• Variable Annuities
• U.S. Treasuries	• Real Estate
• Under the mattress	• Ginnie Mae's

Contrary to popular belief, most bonds (other than government bonds) fall on the risk side. In my humble opinion, you encounter risk any time you put your money some place where the principal can go up and down based on circumstances other than your withdrawals. I have seen many people get into trouble in retirement because they thought their investments were more conservative than they turned out to be.

Let me share a perfect example. Two great people named Ed and Sylvia, who later became clients of our firm, heard me on the radio. They decided to come see me because they feared their retirement plan was on a crash course—and they were right. By the time we met, they were both seventy-two and had been retired for ten years. They had a nice pension, had taken their Social Security at sixty-two, and had a pretty decent nest egg saved up in their 401(k), IRA, and brokerage accounts. At that time, according to their recollection, they had $750,000 saved.

They had met their advisor, Jim, at Ed's former workplace and had been working with him for more than ten years. Initially, Jim had advised them on Ed's 401(k).Eventually, he took over the rest of their accounts. Over their working years, Jim had done well for Ed and Sylvia. He was always available to meet when they needed him. Although their money had gone up and down with the market, overall, with Jim's help, they had accumulated a nice nest egg. So, of course, when Ed and Sylvia were about to retire, they got together with Jim to strategize. Jim's advice was simple: now that they were going to retire, they should reposition and move more funds to bonds, some individual and some bond funds. Most likely, Jim made this suggestion because he believed, like most advisors, that diversification is the key to safety. He advised Ed and Sylvia to keep the rest of their nest egg in diversified stock mutual funds and some individual stocks.

Jim assured them that by putting more money in bonds and keeping the rest well diversified in mutual funds and stocks, they would be in a conservative portfolio and would remain set for life. He assured them that they could take out 4 percent from their portfolio each year and raise that withdrawal by 3 percent each year to keep up with inflation. The plan seemed perfect: the bonds would throw off the income they needed, and the stocks would grow their portfolio to keep up with inflation. Beautifully set up, right? Well, then, you might ask, why were Ed and Sylvia in my office asking for my help?

Let's do a little reality check here. Early into Ed and Sylvia's retirement, many of their bonds were called. This meant they received less income from the new bonds (interest rates had sunk, in case Jim had not noticed). Two years into retirement, Ed and Sylvia needed a car that cost $25,000 and for which they had not been budgeted, so they sold some stock in Ed's 401(k). Ouch! That raised their tax bracket, and what a scathing tax bill they received. To add insult to injury, on the day they redeemed those stocks, the market was down, so they had to sell more shares than they would have if they had sold them the week before. At that point, with less income being generated from their bonds, they needed more money from their stock portfolio, so each year they sold some assets to make up their income deficit.

Ten years into retirement, Ed and Sylvia were deeply concerned about their financial security and fearful they would outlive their money. Though they still liked Jim and trusted his integrity, they were questioning his ability to help them because, thus far, Jim's words of wisdom had been to take out less each month or to just "sit tight and do not worry, because the market will come back—it always does!" I bet you have heard such comments before.

Ed and Sylvia had tired of hearing that same old song with no new results, and so they looked for a second opinion, which happened to be mine. They were right to come see me. Their concerns were on the mark and required immediate attention. When I showed them the reality of their financial situation and deconstructed the numbers, they clearly saw that in order to stop the financial bleeding they would, in fact, have to make some small lifestyle changes as well as some portfolio changes. Only then would they be certain that they would not outlive their money. That said, if they had come to me at the onset of retirement and we had set things up correctly, most likely they would have gone calmly about the business of living their retired life, unencumbered by worries and cutbacks.

The type of plan they had is what I call "one size fits all," but, unfortunately, it was not the right size for them. Now, it is not that Jim is a bad guy. Rather, he is a general practitioner, an accumulation specialist, who helps people try and grow their money, and he works with people of all ages. *If I have taught you anything so far, it should be this: when you get close to or are in retirement, the type of planning required to position your wealth to your retirement advantage is based on an entirely different set of rules than those you followed while employed, and you should be planning accordingly.*

First and foremost, Ed and Sylvia needed to know—based on their own financial DNA—how much money to keep in a safe zone so that they would always have adequate income to maintain their lifestyle, regardless of how the market performed. The only way the one-size-fits-all approach (which puts "some in stocks and some in bonds") works is if market conditions are great. We have not seen much of that lately. Regardless, why should people retire dependent on a capricious market to subsidize their lifestyle choices when, instead, they could have a retirement plan that performs for them in both up and down markets? Why shouldn't they have a plan that they control and that has certainty? All right, I know I am being repetitive, but it is essential you understand that while you and I cannot possibly control the stock market, we can control and follow a plan that clearly lays out the appropriate balance between safety and risk in our own specific circumstances, one that defines our own financial DNA.

A good starting place from which to determine your risk zone is to use the simple rule of a hundred. All you do is take your age and subtract it from a hundred. Whatever is left is the maximum percentage of money you should have exposed to the market. This is just a starting point (by the way, this is not my rule; it's John Bogel's rule, and Bogel is the guru of Vanguard mutual funds). If you realize that you have more risk than you should according to this rule, I encourage you to fix this now before you become the next "should've, could've, would've" person I have to try and talk off the ledge. Please consult the Pyramid of Investing, shown below, so that you can actually see how much risk you are taking.

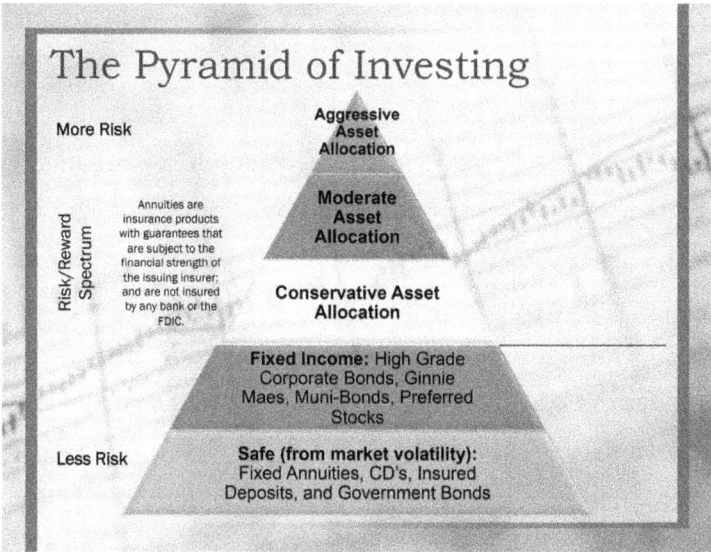

The Pyramid of Investing

More Risk

Aggressive Asset Allocation

Risk/Reward Spectrum

Annuities are insurance products with guarantees that are subject to the financial strength of the issuing insurer; and are not insured by any bank or the FDIC.

Moderate Asset Allocation

Conservative Asset Allocation

Fixed Income: High Grade Corporate Bonds, Ginnie Maes, Muni-Bonds, Preferred Stocks

Less Risk

Safe (from market volatility): Fixed Annuities, CD's, Insured Deposits, and Government Bonds

I want to emphasize something else as well, which is that old habits die hard. If you are like most people, all through your working years you have invested in the market. Changing that mindset does not come easily. Then, of course, you have Wall Street telling you that as long as you diversify between stocks and bonds, everything will come up roses. I say that this is bad advice for someone in the preservation stage of life. While this is not rocket science, you have to know your number—your unique balance between safety and risk—and invest accordingly.

Say you have done it: you have figured out that magic number for you in your specific situation, and you have determined how much of your hard-earned money you should invest in the risk world. If you listen to the average broker, advisor, or Wall Street commercial, each is going to promote investing the same way you did it in the 1990s: through the buy-and-hold method. Well, I strongly disagree with this approach. Given today's circumstances, I believe we must invest differently. If you are fifty years of age or older, you have two enemies—that's right, I said enemies—you must consider when investing.

The first one is time. Do you really have time for the market to recover at this stage of your life? I am fifty-three, and I do not. The other enemy is the stage in the market cycle: we are in a secular bear market cycle. In other words, we are in a long-term cycle in which the market is going to perform badly. During a bear market, the market will occasionally go up, but there will certainly be more downs. Do you like roller-coaster rides? If you do not stop investing your money the Wall Street way, you are going to be taking one. That is how it works in a bear market.

Now, I am going to get political for a moment, but I promise I will keep it short and sweet. Wall Street pundits tell us the market is getting strong and it is a great time to be in it, rah rah rah. Of course the market is going up right now because Mr. Bernanke is printing money at the speed of light. He is manipulating the market, and at some point, that has to stop. Pick your poison. What is the reason why the market will not go up as it did in the 1990s? Is it the inflation that will be caused by all this money being circulated? Is it the rash of problems around the world? Is it the enormous debt that will eventually cause taxes to skyrocket? Or is it the unemployment rate?

I am done with my political tirade, and I hope you get the point. Please know that I could add many more reasons to that list. Even if you are an optimist and you are drinking the Wall Street Kool-Aid, if you start thinking of the topic this way, you might put your glass down. Forget politics; let us take this approach. There is a reason that people look back at market history and say we can learn from it: it is cyclical history. The chart below cannot verify that any more clearly. This chart represents a 113-year look at the Dow Jones stock market index. It verifies that we have gone through repetitive cycles throughout history. Dark gray stands for bear markets; light gray stands for bull markets. Bear markets tend to last longer, and to date, as you see here, the shortest bear market in history lasted sixteen years.

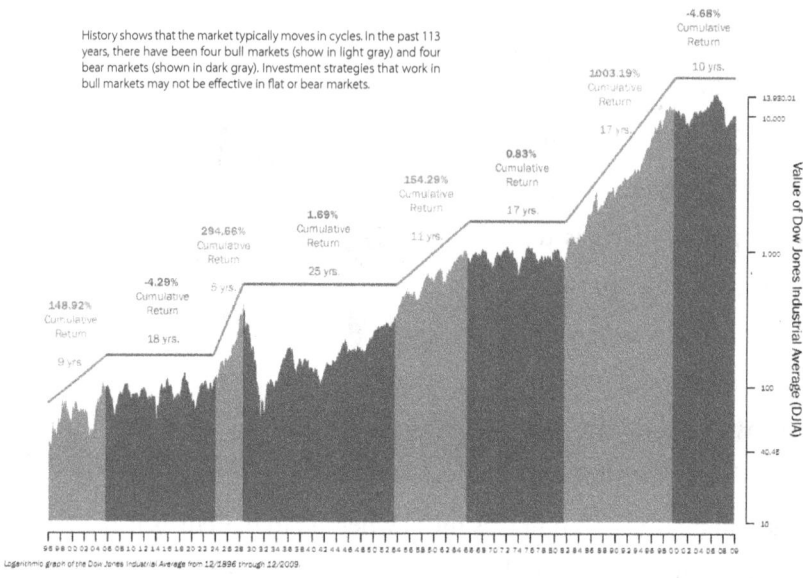

History shows that the market typically moves in cycles. In the past 113 years, there have been four bull markets (show in light gray) and four bear markets (shown in dark gray). Investment strategies that work in bull markets may not be effective in flat or bear markets.

Logarithmic graph of the Dow Jones Industrial Average from 12/1896 through 12/2009.

My point is that if history teaches us anything, it clearly shows us that given normal trends, we are in the midst of a bear market, a long-term, bad, roller-coaster market. This chart shows that natural cycles produce these results. Harry Dent, a brilliant economist and a frequent guest on my weekly radio show, has predicted many of these trends so accurately it gives me goose bumps. He says that aside from politics, normal demographic trends cause these different market cycles. Check Harry's work out. I find him fascinating, and his latest book, *The Great Depression Ahead*, really puts our economic challenges into perspective and helps you plan for the future.

DON'T TRY TO BE BULLISH IN A BEAR MARKET

My point here is that we are clearly in a bear market. In a bear market, if you invest in the same way that you do in a bull market, you are invoking a recipe for disaster. Why? In a bull market, for the most part, the market goes straight up; while there may be some small corrections, it is mostly just peaks. In a bear market, we see lots of peaks and valleys, but mostly valleys. In a bull market, the Wall Street method of buy and hold works like a charm. Buy a stock or a mutual fund, hold on to it, and watch as, like magic, it goes up and up. Let's take the bull run of the 1990s as an example. The tech revolution, the dawn of the Internet, the period of time when we all began to invest in the market in earnest, was such a good time that no matter what you bought, you were practically destined to make money. You could have blindfolded yourself, thrown darts against a wall of a thousand different stock picks, and probably could not have hit a loser. If you employed dollar-cost averaging, buying the same stock or mutual fund consistently at different prices, both high and low, you made out like a bandit. If you were fortunate enough to retire at that time, you could withdraw high percentages from your portfolio and still make money in those times. The bottom line is, if your investment correlated to the market, you did well with buy and hold. The market went up, so you went up. Simple.

In a bear market, does the market go straight up? Absolutely not. So, if you use the same methods today that worked in the '90s, you will have problems. Wall Street and most advisors still promote those same methods. They want you to buy something and just let it ride. When the market goes up, that is great, but when the market goes down, you go down with it. If you are retired, do you really want to play that game? Historians and economists are calling the last decade a "lost decade" in the market, because if you did things the buy-and-hold way, if you got in and stayed in, you did not make a penny; in fact, you probably lost money. If you retired into this market, as Ed and Sylvia did, and needed that money to subsidize your lifestyle, now you are probably in some trouble. Taking money out of a market on a consistent basis, or reverse dollar-cost averaging, is a nightmare in a bear market. Think about that. If you are retired and you lose money that you cannot replace with a paycheck, what do you do? I know…Wall Street will give it back to you. Except that will not actually happen.

Here is what you can do: invest your money appropriately for the present market condition. The definition of insanity is doing the same thing over and over again and expecting different results. Today, I see that all the time. People are making investments in the market that are correlated to the major market indices—the Dow Jones, S&P, and the Russell 2000—and expecting to make and keep gains in this bear market. Wall Street keeps giving them the hype, and they keep on believing it. You know, when people come into my office, I ask them how they did in the market in 2008, or over the past decade. If they tell me "good" or that they went down like everybody else, I know one of two things is going to happen. Either it is going to be a really short visit because the potential client is too stuck in his or her ways to be open to change, or this meeting will be eye opening and life changing for him or her in terms of a retirement future. The point is that not everyone lost money in 2008 or even over the last ten years. People who invested correctly for the times made money. In a bear market, this is more challenging, but if you actively manage your account and are prepared with strategies to make money when the market goes up as well as when it goes down, there is money to be had in even a bear market.

So, how are you invested? If, the last time you went to see your financial person after a market downturn, he or she said something like this to you, "I've got good news and bad news; the bad news is the market indices went down 28 percent, but the good news is you went down less!", do not be in too big a hurry to give that person a raise. If he or she explained that you are invested in a total-return or buy-and-hold strategy, you had better buckle your seat belt because you are destined to go up and down with the market. Now on the other hand, if you are in actively managed strategies, you have probably made some money, since even if the market goes down, you have been positioned to make a return. This is what is known as absolute return strategies. Again, while you cannot control the ups and downs of the market, you can control the methods you use to invest in the market. Remember, focus on what you can control. Do not risk what you cannot afford to lose!

FEES

Get the Most Bang for the Buck

FEES

Get the Most Bang for the Buck

*Now I get docked 10 to 20 percent of my appearance fee
if I do not yell at some people and break at least one racket.*

—JOHN McENROE

Even if you were not a tennis fan during the late '70s and '80s, you have probably heard of John McEnroe's notorious tantrums on the tennis court, which are legendary. Of course, it helped that he was a great player too. Now an engaging tennis commentator, McEnroe's quip does not seem too far from the truth of what people might sneak into one of his contract's today just to see a replay of those fiery displays that erupted in reaction to perceived bad calls. And the consensus was, more times than not, that McEnroe was right about the call. He had extraordinary, eagle-eyed vision. While I am not trying to excuse his bad behavior, I do wish to note that too many bad calls could cost someone a championship and the winner's purse. If you will indulge me as I open this chapter with a courtside comment, you will be rewarded. It is designed to get your wheels turning about fees, expectations, and penalties. Plus, it will not hurt to inject a bit of McEnroe's intensity and aggression in calling out the fine print of your investments. It is your retirement purse that is on the dotted line, after all.

In terms of investing, fees are an area that you can control, but you have to be aggressive about accounting for every single one. I do not pretend to understand why many otherwise smart people I have met have no idea of the fees they are paying on their investments. At this point, a little disclaimer is in order: I am partly paid by fees, so I am certainly not against them. However, I cannot stress enough how important it is for you to get a full understanding and disclosure of the fees you are paying so that you know you are getting the most bang for your buck.

I do not understand why the above is not a given. If you go out and make a purchase, whether it is of a car or a dishwasher, like most of us you probably do your due diligence and make sure you get the most value for your dollar. Right? You get the CARFAX or read consumer reports or reviews. That is totally logical. Yet, when it comes to investing their life savings, most people I talk to do not investigate with the same level of due diligence. Why not? You need to start now. Granted, most people feel overwhelmed by the challenges of managing their money; they would rather just put their trust in an advisor. You can do that if you want to but remember that if it goes badly, the only one who loses is you. This is an area in which you definitely have control, and I strongly encourage you to take it.

You can and should hold your advisor accountable for the full disclosure of fees, returns, and different options. Certainly, you should make sure that your advisor has explained in a very clear and logical way why he or she is making those specific recommendations for you. Today, the average person has many options. In the retail world of mutual funds and load funds you can choose among different share classes (typically A, B, and C shares). There are pros and cons to each one depending upon your specific circumstances.

For example, an A-share mutual fund has an upfront load. A load is the commission you pay to buy the fund. A-share mutual fund loads can range from 3 percent on bond funds to 5.25 percent on stock funds and specialty funds. All mutual funds, including no-load funds, have an expense ratio. An expense ratio is what the money management firm charges a client for the management of the fund. These fees can be all over the place and range from very low to painfully high charges. Although A-shares may come with an upfront commission, they typically offer the lowest ongoing expense ratio. Thus, the A-share purchase option is often your best buy.

Two share classes that make little sense are B-shares and C-shares. B-shares look like no-load funds, but they come with a catch. B-shares typically have higher expense ratios, which help mutual fund companies recapture the commissions they paid to the selling broker. C-shares are not much better. In these cases, companies add the commission on to the expense ratio. If your money management firm charges a fee of 1 percent, and your advisor sells you C-shares and also charges you a 1 percent fee, that results in an annual fee of 2 percent. C-shares may make sense in the short term, but realistically, as a retiree, you should not be investing in short-term funds.

Fees: Gains and Losses

- According to Morningstar, the average mutual fund has a fee of 1.31 percent. That is before we look at any hidden fees or what you are paying your broker. To keep things simple, let us assume you are not paying what most people are and your average total fees are only 1.25 percent.
- If your mutual fund/ETF/stock portfolio has a 1.25 percent annual fee, that fee not only reduces your gains but also compounds your losses. Have you ever thought about that?
- If your mutual fund/ETF/stock portfolio makes money:
  - 5 percent return - 1.25 percent fee = you keep only **75 percent** of the gain
  - 7.5 percent return - 1.25 percent fee = you keep only **83 percent** of the gain
  - 10 percent return - 1.25 percent fee = you keep only **87.5 percent** of the gain
- If your mutual fund/ETF/stock portfolio loses money:
  - 5 percent loss - 1.25 percent fee = 125 percent total loss to you
  - 7.5 percent loss - 1.25 percent fee = 117.5 percent total loss to you
  - 10 percent loss - 1.25 percent fee = 112.5 percent total loss to you
- Thus, if your fund averages a 10 percent return per year (a highly unrealistic number), you are keeping 87.5 percent of the gain and accepting more than 100 percent of the risk.
- How does that make you feel?

Personally, I am not a fan of retail mutual funds for many reasons. The biggest reason I am against them is that these funds have many fees disclosed in the prospectus along with a ton of fees that the SEC does not require the company to disclose. That takes place in that huge, boring prospectus that nobody really reads anyway. In my opinion, you will usually get more bang for your buck with no-load funds or exchange-traded funds (ETFs). A simple definition of an ETF is that it is a security that tracks an index like a no-load mutual fund but trades like a stock on the exchange. An ETF is more liquid and usually less expensive than even no-load mutual funds.

Today, even the smaller investor can get into institutional investing. This has typically been the primary investing venue for the big boys, but investment advisors can now make this available to the average investor. A Series 65 advisor, such as me, can work in the institutional world instead of the retail world, just like the big wire houses, Morgan Stanley, Merrill Lynch, and so forth. This is how I, as a Series 65 advisor, choose to work with my clients when we manage money, since the advantages are huge: there are far fewer fees than mutual funds incur, more active management (which usually leads to better returns), and more liquidity.

Another vehicle to investigate closely is your 401(k). Be aware that your 401(k) has fees that are disclosed as well as fees that are not. Please make sure you do your best to examine all your options within that 401(k) so you can make the best choices for yourself. Today, the government has begun to require 401(k) providers to reveal their fees, but such information is still difficult for the average investor to uncover. It is so important for you to get a handle on this because, if you are like most people today, your 401(k) stands in place of a guaranteed pension; it is probably a very big part of your retirement nest egg. Guess what? You are the only one managing it. This is a huge ball in your court.

X-RAY YOUR INVESTMENTS

At my firm a very big service we render to our clients is what we call the "X-ray for your 401(k)." We dig into it, closely examine it, expose both the fees and returns, and evaluate the amount of risk you are taking. I strongly recommend that you do the same. If your advisor is not offering this service to you, this absence may be a big indication that you are not working with the right individual.

A useful do-it-yourself tool you can use to check out your 401(k) can be found on the website www.brightscope.com

A useful do-it-yourself tool you can use to check out your 401(k) can be found on the website www.brightscope.com. The creator of this site, Mike Alfred, is a great advocate for people on this 401(k) issue. I commend all he has done to expose the fees within these plans and his relentless efforts to convince the government to require that these fees be exposed. Mike has been a great guest on my radio show.

I also want to warn you about variable annuities. Unless you have a no-load variable annuity (and I bet your broker is not telling you about those), what you do have are excessive fees. Variable annuities are, in the simplest terms, retail mutual funds (also known as subaccounts in the variable annuity) that are exposed to the market volatility, along with all the corresponding high fees that are both disclosed and undisclosed, wrapped inside an insurance product. That means the inclusion of even more fees: mortality fees, expense fees, and administrative fees. These can add up; I have seen variable annuities with fees as high as 3 to 5 percent of the account value. Today, these products have additional benefits or riders that you can add on—with more fees—to guarantee death benefits and living benefits. On the surface, they sound great, and in some circumstances, since every situation is different, they make sense. Most often, they are very confusing and do not correspond to what people think they are getting.

Again, my mission is to encourage you to take control of your money and to ensure that you understand what kinds of investments you have and their role in your overall retirement plan. One of my favorite challenges to audiences at my public workshops and my weekly radio show is an open invitation for anyone to come to my office for a personalized X-ray of his or her investment vehicles, especially variable annuities. In the case of a variable annuity, conducting the X-ray consists of getting a representative from the client's insurance company on the speakerphone. Then, I proceed to ask pertinent and detailed questions to ensure that the client understands exactly what he or she has. This is an eye-opening experience for nine out of ten people who participate. Most people, bright people, do not know what they really own when they have a variable annuity because these annuities are so darn complicated. With thirty-plus years in the business, I know the questions to ask that can give people greater knowledge of, and insight into, the working parts of this investment vehicle. In my opinion, it is of the upmost importance that you understand what you have. This is a critical component of your nest egg, and the choice of where to invest your money is entirely up to you. Be relentless in uncovering the details.

In summary, you cannot control the market, but you can control how much you put in it, how you choose to invest in it, and the fees you pay. Again, stop worrying about what you cannot control. Instead, control what you can, since the decisions that you make will have a huge impact on your retirement. Be aggressive in your questions and settle for nothing less than clear and transparent answers that result in the full disclosure of all pertinent details and fees. These fees can certainly add up and will diminish your retirement portfolio if you are not paying attention.

INCOME PLANNING
THE RIGHT WAY

Income Planning the Right Way

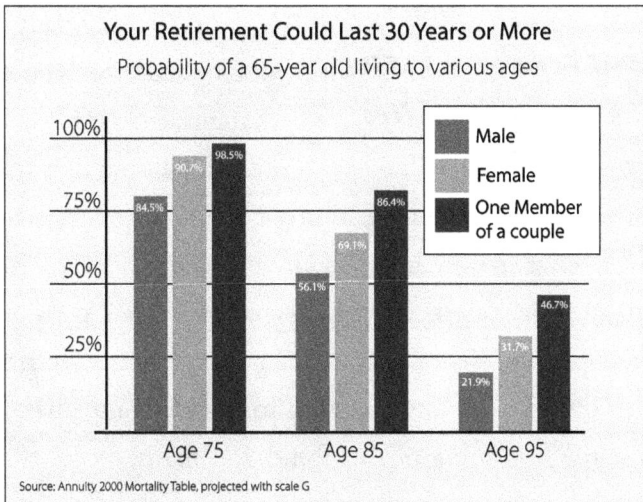

Your Retirement Could Last 30 Years or More
Probability of a 65-year old living to various ages

	Age 75	Age 85	Age 95
Male	84.5%	56.1%	21.9%
Female	90.7%	69.1%	31.7%
One Member of a couple	98.5%	86.4%	46.7%

Source: Annuity 2000 Mortality Table, projected with scale G

When people begin to consider their retirement life, probably the greatest fear most of them have is that they will outlive their money. Quite frankly, this is a valid concern and will be a real danger if it is not part of your preservation plan.

According to the Government Accountability Office (GAO) report of August 2011, "Today, a husband and wife both aged sixty-five have approximately a 47 percent chance that at least one of them will live to his or her ninetieth birthday and a 20 percent chance of living to his or her ninety-fifth birthday."

Knowing that you have a high probability for a longer life, please do not bury your fears and what-ifs under the sand alongside the proverbial ostrich's head. Instead, accept this as a very real threat to your retirement stability and incorporate strategies to address it in your retirement planning. If you put together a solid plan that guarantees you reliable, steady income that takes into account the effects of inflation and three possible decades more of good living, you will be able to retire that fear once and for all.

Let's face it. The challenges surrounding our retirement income require proactive solutions. We have already established that we live in what is essentially a pensionless society. The days of that nice, guaranteed, defined-benefit pension that you could

At what age should you take Social Security?

count on when you retired are mostly gone. Few people have these any more. Even if you do, how solid is your pension today? Recently, both Ford and GM have been making changes in their pension plans, offering people options of lump-sum payouts or transferring their payouts to immediate annuities with insurance companies. I think this is just the beginning of this trend and many more will follow suit.

Social Security, if you get it, and I think we all will to some extent, is not enough to retire on. It was never intended to be more than 40 percent of your retirement income in the first place. However, at what age you should take it is still an important consideration for your planning. An experienced retirement and income planner will explore these options with you. With the advances of modern medicine, we are living longer, which means we have to plan for longer life expectancies. It is very possible that if you retire at sixty-five you can live thirty or more years in retirement without a paycheck. How are you going to do that?

HAVE A PLAN TO REPLACE THAT PAYCHECK FOR THE NEXT THIRTY-PLUS YEARS

My point in all this is that if you want to be assured you will not outlive your money, you have to take control and make certain you have an income plan that is structured properly to give you a certainty of income that will endure throughout your lifetime. You have to have a plan in place that will replace that paycheck for the next thirty to forty years. Most people are of the mindset that they just need to accumulate a certain amount of money and draw out a certain percentage of that amount throughout retirement, and all will be well. Well, that is partially true. You do have to save and accumulate a nest egg to draw from, and obviously the more you accumulate the better. However, where you invest that nest egg, how much you withdraw, and when you withdraw it are crucial considerations in determining the success of that income plan.

Over the years, a big mistake I have seen people make is missing this important step in the planning process. As a result, they are financially devastated. It is so incredibly sad to meet people who worked hard all their lives, saved a nice nest egg, and then lost most of it because of poor or no income planning. A huge part of what I do every day is design income plans so that this does not happen to my clients. Together, based on their specific goals and circumstances, we build an income plan based on certainty, not just a wing and a prayer. This idea is worth repeating again because it is so important. **In your working years, in the accumulation phase, you should be focused on growing and growing that nest egg. In the preservation phase of your life, you should focus on keeping that nest egg, growing it safely, and making sure it creates guaranteed, reliable streams of income.** This is the area in which you really see differences between an advisor who specializes in accumulation and an advisor who specializes in preservation and income distribution in terms of wealth management. How these advisors approach creating that income plan will be critically different. I maintain that doing income planning incorrectly can make or break you.

So, what is the right way and what is the wrong way, at least according to me? Well, first you have to know your numbers. How much do you need to finance your lifestyle? We have already done this work in previous chapters, and it bears repeating. This number drives your plan, so it needs to be carefully and accurately calculated. Break it down into monthly needs and wants. What do your necessities cost you each month, and what do the discretionary expenses cost? Once you have a solid number, determine how much you have coming in each month from fixed sources of income. The variance between the two is the amount that you need to supplement from your nest egg. Of course, you need to factor inflation into that number as well.

The above is always the critical starting point. So many people have what I call one-size-fits-all plans, and they have no true idea of what their number is. At best, they have a guesstimate, or they pick an arbitrary number out of thin air that they think will cover expenses each month. The usual type of income plan that I see (if clients even have one) is one in which the advisor has taken the assets and diversified them to make sure that the client spreads out risk between bonds, which are "safe" and great for income, and stocks, so that the money grows in order to keep up with inflation. Usually, the advisor tells the client not to take out more than 4 percent per year. Ed and Sylvia's portfolio, as I described it to you earlier, was the epitome of the average accumulation specialist's methods. In the '90s, when the stock market was great, this type of plan was fine, but today the stock market is not great, and this is not fine. Quite frankly, whether the market is good or bad, unless you have a crystal ball and know for certain what is going to happen to the money you have at risk in stocks and bonds, this simply is not the way to plan. Imagine if your bosses had told you in your working years that they were going to give you a paycheck that was based on the performance of the market. I am sure you would have said, "Wait a minute, you can't do that!" Think about it; that is what you are doing with your life savings if you leave the money invested in stocks and bonds, where the value can go up and down.

LADDER YOUR INVESTMENTS FOR INCOME CERTAINTY

You can control this because you, as the CEO of your money, get to decide where to put it. My clients have customized, structured, and scheduled income plans so that whether the market is up or down, they get the money they planned to get. For them, my team and I do income laddering. We structure a plan that provides our clients with a certain amount of income, and they know exactly where it is coming from. It is all laid out in black and white. Once we know what they need to fund their lifestyle choices, we create reliable income streams that use different types of safe income-generating vehicles. You should not invest income that you need in retirement in places where you can only hope for the right outcome. After all, you cannot pay your bills with hope. You have to have a plan of certainty.

Obviously, you have to have realistic expectations in the first place. However, once you do have that realistic number, I am telling you, as a preservation and income-planning specialist, there are tools you can use to put together an income plan of certainty. This is definitely something you need to have, and whether or not you have it is within your control. If you do not know exactly how and where your income is coming from, how long it is guaranteed to last, or what the plan for keeping up with inflation is, you do not have an income plan and in my opinion it is imperative that you make some changes!

Earlier, I discussed the pyramid of investing and included a graphic that shows you that the higher up the pyramid you go, the riskier your investments become. Below, I have included a match-up between an expense matrix and the pyramid of investing. It will show you how, in not only in my opinion, but in Alicia Munnell's, the head of the Center For Retirement Research at Boston College, your money should be invested to match certain expenses. I hope you take this point to heart because a mistake with your money at this stage of life does not afford you a second chance; when that money is gone, it is gone. You do not have time to work and replace it.

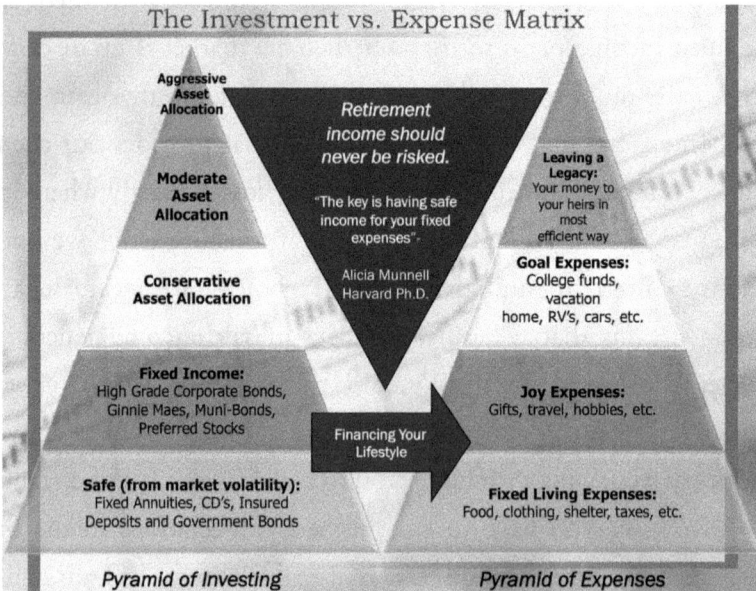

The Investment vs. Expense Matrix

Aggressive Asset Allocation

Moderate Asset Allocation

Conservative Asset Allocation

Retirement income should never be risked.

"The key is having safe income for your fixed expenses"-

Alicia Munnell Harvard Ph.D.

Leaving a Legacy: Your money to your heirs in most efficient way

Goal Expenses: College funds, vacation home, RV's, cars, etc.

Fixed Income: High Grade Corporate Bonds, Ginnie Maes, Muni-Bonds, Preferred Stocks

Financing Your Lifestyle

Joy Expenses: Gifts, travel, hobbies, etc.

Safe (from market volatility): Fixed Annuities, CD's, Insured Deposits and Government Bonds

Fixed Living Expenses: Food, clothing, shelter, taxes, etc.

Pyramid of Investing   Pyramid of Expenses

Unfortunately, today many older people are working in places such as Wal-Mart, not because they miss work but because they did not have a realistic income plan. When the market blew up in 2008, so did their plan. I bet their advisors were really nice and felt really bad, but that did not replace what these people lost.

You can hope you will be able to maintain your lifestyle in retirement, or you can be certain that you will. The bottom line is that this choice is yours. I suggest that at this stage of your life, certainty is the ticket. Certainty is the way to have peace of mind in good and bad economies. With a strong, solid income plan, you have certainty as well as flexibility. This is a change in mindset that you really should embrace.

CONTROLLING WHAT YOU CAN IN UNCERTAIN TIMES

CONTROLLING WHAT YOU CAN IN UNCERTAIN TIMES

By now, I trust you have realized that focusing on what you can control has a direct and immediate effect on your money. Ultimately, it determines the lifestyle that you will be able to enjoy throughout your retirement. So, how can you be sure that you are maximizing that control and doing the best you can for your future?

CHOOSE A WINNING TEAM OF FINANCIAL EXPERTS

First and foremost, I think it is important to pick a winning team. Of course, you can do it alone, but the fact is that the rules of the game are changing rapidly. You need, and should have, trusted guides who focus on solving the types of problems that you are facing. Clearly, it is important to recognize what stage of life you are in with regard to your money, because the advisor you pick should be a specialist in the specific financial stage on which you are focusing. Again, if you are within ten years of retirement or are already retired, you are either in, or transitioning into, the second financial stage, the preservation and income-distribution stage. In the preservation and income-distribution stage, your main focus should be protecting the money that you cannot afford to lose and making sure that it grows safely and securely. This way, you can live your life independently on your own terms.

So, let's put together your checklist for assembling the right team. Let's talk about the advisor first. Again, you need a specialist in this phase. How do you know if the person you are considering is a specialist? She or he should be, first of all, fully licensed. By this I mean both fully licensed on the insurance side of things and on the investment side of things, since the key to developing a good, well-balanced retirement plan is being able to integrate the safe world and the risk world strategically so they are compatible with your financial DNA. It is also advisable to work with someone who is independent. An independent advisor does not work with one specific insurance company or one specific wire house. As a result, he or she has no quotas to meet or proprietary products to peddle. Once he or she has designed the right plan with this structure, he or she will be able to bring you the entire universe of investment vehicles and options, a selection from which you can pick and choose what is going to be most appropriate for your particular circumstances. I also think it is in your best interests to work with an investment advisor rather than a broker because an investment advisor is held to a higher level of accountability, as I mentioned earlier. In addition, the fees are more transparent and you encounter less potential for a conflict of interest. You can have more reassurance that you are getting the most bang for your buck.

Equally important in making your choice is determining what kind of education the advisor has had in the past and what he or she is doing to keep informed and up-to-date in the areas that could impact the success of your retirement plan. Make sure that your advisor is an expert in retirement and tax planning, which is key because most of your money is probably in a retirement account, and if that is not handled correctly, that retirement nest egg may crack and create a huge tax bomb for you and your heirs.

Because the Internal Revenue is forever changing its tax laws, and this is so crucial to the success of my clients' retirement plans, I am a Master Elite IRA Advisor. As I mentioned before, I am mentored on an extensive, intensive, and ongoing basis by Ed Slott, the foremost authority on retirement tax planning and distribution planning.

When interviewing a potential advisor, do not be afraid to ask by whom he or she has been trained in this area or what type of education he or she has received in this area.

To reiterate, remember to ask the "Ten Questions to Ask Your Financial Advisor" in order to be sure the advisor is an expert in this area and can answer those questions quickly, correctly, and with confidence. Having a tax-efficient plan is pertinent to the success of your retirement, so your advisor needs to be proficient in this area. When interviewing potential advisors, ask them what they are going to require from you to put together a plan. If they do not require your tax return, you should see a big red flag. This means that they do not see how important it is to incorporate tax planning into your overall retirement plan.

Another technique that is crucial to the success of your retirement plan is incorporating a plan that covers a catastrophic illness. As I discussed earlier, there are many innovative strategies you can use to help plan for the event of a catastrophic illness. Is the advisor talking to you about the importance of including this in your overall plan? If not, that is another red flag. If so, how educated is the advisor in this area? For example, quite frequently I take continuing education courses on long-term care to keep abreast of the new trends and help myself in advising my clients.

Do the advisor candidates have education simply regarding investment products, or do they have continued education about retirement and income planning? Are they truly retirement and income planners, or do they just have knowledge about products? A true retirement and income planner has the capacity to lay out an income plan that shows you with certainty how and where you will receive necessary income for the rest of your life. Our clients receive an income plan as part of their overall plan, and they can identify how and where they will get their income for the rest of their lives. That is a must in a solid retirement plan. As I pointed out earlier in this book, you cannot have a plan based on hope; it must be based on certainty. When it comes to your income, certainty has to be absolute. This takes a specific skill set, and not all advisors are equipped with these skills. Make sure that you work with a specialist who does have this skill set.

It is very important that your advisor is educated in the appropriate areas. However, while someone can have all the education in the world, if he or she cannot sit down with you, listen, and ask the right questions to help you carefully develop what your plan is going to look like in retirement, he or she is useless. I have seen many CFPs, many people with fancy letters after their names, who do not know how to listen. Often they sit there, barely hearing what you have to say, and then want to tell you everything that they can do. You need an advisor who will really listen and ask the appropriate questions, someone who is willing to take the time to understand your concerns, so that he or she can put together a comprehensive retirement plan that will guide you down the path you want to take. What do you want your retirement to look like? What is it going to cost to finance that retirement?

After you have asked all the questions, after the advisor has listened, and after the advisor has led the mission to capture the picture of your ideal retirement, it is important that the advisor can articulate back to you very, very clearly what he or she heard you say. If you find that communication is broken down at that point, that person is not the right advisor for you. A good advisor should view her or his role as one in which he or she can educate you in the areas you can control, based upon where you want to go and what you want your life to be like, and then guide you down your chosen path. However, the advisor has to partner with you each step of the way so that you feel in control of your money. I think it is very important that the advisor should willingly provide proof for all his or her suggestions and show you in black and white why he or she is making suggestions and why those suggestions work in your plan. When you are choosing an advisor, it is absolutely appropriate to expect that proof.

Do not be hesitant or timid to do your homework and find out about the advisor's background; ask for and call his or her references. Take the time to understand who this person is, and make sure you have made a great choice. This is your hard-earned money; you do not get second chances on this. Does this advisor write articles for magazines, journals, or newspapers on topics that display his or her expertise? Has he or she written a book? Again, does he or she invest in professional knowledge, and if so, how often? Who are the other experts with whom he or she works? Of what organizations is he or she a member? What do his or her other clients say?

All of the answers to these questions are important in accomplishing the ultimate goal: empowering you to make the right decisions so you can be in control of your money. At the end of the day, you are the CEO of your money, and what you control will greatly affect the lifestyle you will be able to afford.

A pivotal role of the right advisor should be that of your lead relationship manager. He or she will not only be the person who designs your plan and who picks and chooses the right products for your plan, but he or she will also be the one who puts together that team of experts to complete your estate plan. A comprehensive estate plan requires the expertise of an estate-planning attorney, and a great advisor will already be collaborating with the right estate-planning attorney. If you are already in retirement, the right type of estate-planning attorney should be someone who specializes in that area and who specifically works with your age group. Your advisor should have those relationships in place if he or she is in the business of putting together plans for people, since putting the whole package together requires the expertise of many specialties. An advisor who is just selling products may not have these kinds of relationships or may not understand the importance of having an estate plan that reinforces and complements the other components of the plan he or she has developed.

In our practice we insist on excellence all the way around. If we develop a great financial plan and it fails on the estate-planning side of things, we have not done our job. That is just unacceptable. We are not attorneys. I always joke with clients that I know just enough to be dangerous. However, I know enough to go out and find very competent attorneys who understand what a good estate plan is and understand how to structure passing on retirement accounts in a tax-efficient manner. A good estate-planning attorney understands how to use the right language and will set up powers of attorney for finance and health care. That way, if there is a catastrophic illness, our clients have the ability to protect their money for their loved ones. We have a team of attorneys who are experts in these areas.

Sometimes, as the relationship manager, I work with clients who have their own trusted estate-planning attorney. As a manager of relationships, a good advisor is going to interview the estate-planning attorney, make sure that he or she is a solid part of the team, and be willing to work with that person. The estate-planning attorney should be willing to work in conjunction with the advisor too. If not, he or she is probably not going to be a good part of the team.

When it is time to select a CPA or a tax preparation expert, again, your advisor should have recommendations for individuals who are willing to work in conjunction with the team. Earlier in this book, I discussed how your CPA's role generally includes making sure that you are compliant and that you pay the right amount of taxes. His or her role is not necessarily to make recommendations regarding investments that control your taxes, since that is more properly the role of the advisor. However, when the CPA and advisor work in conjunction, you end up having a plan on steroids, since the CPA is the one who keeps current on the latest tax rules. When I have recommendations about buying or selling stocks to harvest losses, or anything pertaining to taxes, I want to work with a confident CPA, run that by him or her, and make sure that my recommendations are absolutely correct. A good CPA wants to work in conjunction with an advisor. An appropriate CPA for someone at this stage of retirement, again, is someone who specifically focuses his or her practice on working with people who are retired or about to be. Your potential advisor, who is serving as your relationship manager, should arm your team with the appropriate estate-planning attorney and the appropriate CPA. Again, if you have your own trusted CPA with whom you have a great relationship, a good advisor is going to reach out and form a relationship with that CPA; the advisor will want to interview that CPA to make sure that he or she is competent and that the two can work together, of course, but the advisor should be willing to work with the CPA. On the other side of things, a good CPA is going to see the importance of working together strategically, as a team, to achieve the best results for the client.

The bottom line is, be smart, trust your feelings, and know that you are in control of the experts you pick to be on your winning team. Do your due diligence and make sure that you get the biggest possible bang for your buck.

Checklist for Finding the Right Advisor

✓ Fully Licensed in insurance and investment services to ensure a balanced plan

✓ Specialist for your specific financial stage of life

✓ Independent advisor rather than broker for highest accountability

✓ Proficient and current in retirement and tax planning regulations

✓ Dedicated to continuing education in all areas of his or her expertise

✓ Incorporates holistic plans that include defensive strategies in the event of a healthcare crisis

✓ Strongly listens to your goals and concerns

✓ Transparent and willing to demonstrate why his/her recommendations will work best for you

✓ Passes your due diligence on background, reference checks, and organization memberships

✓ Proof of expertise: books, written articles, publications

✓ Strong collaborator with the right network of experts to complete your team (attorneys, accountants, etc.)

THE LAST WORD...

Congratulations! You now have the tools to empower yourself to take control of your retirement. It is time to take action.

Every corner of the world is confronted by uncertain economies, changing climates, acts of violence, diseases, and crises of all sorts. We cannot change these storms, but, as this book has shown, you can create calm in the midst of it all with a secure retirement plan.

You are the CEO of your money. Do not sit on the sidelines; take this knowledge and apply it. Assemble that great team and work together to develop a plan that will effectively protect your health, your wealth, and your legacy. Start implementing those strategies so that you can truly live your life independently and on your own terms—with certainty.

WEBSITES AND BUDGET TOOLS YOU CAN USE

Useful Websites and Links

PSP & Associates, website for Phillis Sax Pilvinis	www.pspassoc.com
Ed Slott IRA tax and distribution planning website	www.irahelp.com
Do-it-yourself tool to analyze your 401(K)	www.brightscope.com
Social Security Administration	www.socialsecurity.gov/onlineservices/
Safe money vehicle information	www.safemoneyplaces.com
Broker check website	www.finra.org
Investment advisor website	www.sec.gov/investor/brokers.htm
Veteran Aid	www.veteranaid.org

BUDGET WORKSHEET

Monthly expenses at the time of retirement, and future decreases

Year	Amount	Amount decrease
Primary mortgage	$_____	$_____
Other mortgages	$_____	$_____
Taxes & insurance	$_____	$_____
HOA	$_____	$_____
Lawn maintenance	$_____	$_____
Repairs	$_____	$_____
Utilities (water, electricity, gas, etc.) (phone, cell, cable, Internet, etc.)	$_____	$_____
Credit card payments	$_____	$_____
Car payments	$_____	$_____
Insurance	$_____	$_____
Fuel	$_____	$_____
Repairs	$_____	$_____
RV, boat, ATV, etc.	$_____	$_____
Recreation vehicle insurance	$_____	$_____
Groceries	$_____	$_____

Resturants	$_____	$_____
Medical insurance	$_____	$_____
Life insurance	$_____	$_____
LTC insurance	$_____	$_____
Prescriptions	$_____	$_____
Clothing & misc.	$_____	$_____
Travel	$_____	$_____
Recreation	$_____	$_____
Miscellaneous	$_____	$_____
Debt Service	$_____	$_____
Other	$_____	$_____
Total	**$_____**	**$_____**

PHILLIS SAX PILVINIS

President and Founder, PSP & Associates
and PSP Financial Services LLC

A veteran and a pioneer of the financial services industry, Phillis Sax Pilvinis, CRPC®, founder of PSP & Associates, has been assisting baby boomers and retirees in the greater Phoenix and surrounding area for more than a decade. She specializes in retirement and income planning for individuals and their families and considers herself a "preservation specialist" when dealing with life savings.

Phillis is a popular radio show host, published author, and national presenter on the topics of income planning, 401(k) rollovers, and advanced IRA tax reduction strategies. Phillis educates area residents on comprehensive estate and retirement planning issues, helping them avoid the hardships that may come with an underplanned or unplanned retirement. Additionally, she has instructed hundreds of other financial service professionals on how to assist retiring boomers with the transition from the working years to the retirement years, as well as assisting retirees with proper income planning.

Phillis has not only become a successful business professional in Arizona, as featured in *Forbes* magazine, but she has also made great strides nationally as a woman in finance. She was named as a finalist in the top five advisor-of-the-year awards and is frequently asked to share her story at various industry events.

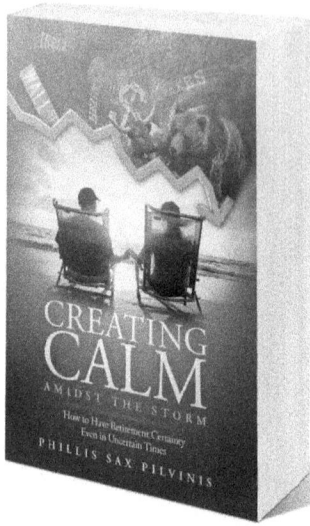

How can you use this book?

MOTIVATE

EDUCATE

THANK

INSPIRE

PROMOTE

CONNECT

Why have a custom version of *Creating Calm Amidst the Storm?*

- Build personal bonds with customers, prospects, employees, donors, and key constituencies

- Develop a long-lasting reminder of your event, milestone, or celebration

- Provide a keepsake that inspires change in behavior and change in lives

- Deliver the ultimate "thank you" gift that remains on coffee tables and bookshelves

- Generate the "wow" factor

Books are thoughtful gifts that provide a genuine sentiment that other promotional items cannot express. They promote employee discussions and interaction, reinforce an event's meaning or location, and they make a lasting impression. Use your book to say "Thank You" and show people that you care.

www.ingramcontent.com/pod-product-compliance
Lightning Source LLC
Chambersburg PA
CBHW050509210326
41521CB00011B/2390